EVENTS & OUTCOMES
THE SLAVE TRADE

TOM MONAGHAN

RAINTREE
STECK-VAUGHN
PUBLISHERS

A Harcourt Company

Austin   New York
www.raintreesteckvaughn.com

First published 2003 by Raintree Steck-Vaughn
Publishers, an imprint of Steck-Vaughn Company

© Evans Brothers Limited 2002

Library of Congress Cataloging-in-Publication Data
is available upon request

ISBN 0-7398-5802-5

Printed in Spain. Bound in the United States.

1 2 3 4 5 6 7 8 9 0 LB 06 05 04 03 02

Edited by Rachel Norridge
Designed by Neil Sayer
Maps by Tim Smith
Consultant: Dr Kevin Shillington

Acknowledgments

Cover The Bridgeman Art Library **Background image** the art archive **p. 6** the art archive **p. 7** (top) Mary Evans Picture Library (bottom) Peter Newark's American Pictures **p. 8** the art archive **p. 9** The Bridgeman Art Library **p. 11** (top) the art archive (bottom) Mary Evans Picture Library **p. 12** the art archive **p. 14** (middle) Mary Evans Picture Library (bottom) The Bridgeman Art Library **p. 15** Mary Evans Picture Library **p. 16** (top) Mary Evans Picture Library (bottom) the art archive **p. 17** (top) Mary Evans Picture Library (bottom) The Bridgeman Art Library **p. 18** (top) the art archive (bottom) The Bridgeman Art Library **p. 19** The Bridgeman Art Library **p. 20** Mary Evans Picture Library **p. 21** (top) Mary Evans Picture Library (bottom) The Bridgeman Art Library **p. 22** (top) Peter Newark's American Pictures (bottom) Topham Picturepoint **p. 23** (top) Mary Evans Picture Library (bottom) Peter Newark's American Pictures **p. 24** Mary Evans Picture Library **p. 25** Mary Evans Picture Library **p. 26** the art archive **p. 27** The Bridgeman Art Library **p. 28** The Bridgeman Art Library **p. 29** Mary Evans Picture Library **p. 30** Mary Evans Picture Library **p. 32** Mary Evans Picture Library **p. 33** Peter Newark's American Pictures **p. 34** Peter Newark's American Pictures **p. 35** Peter Newark's American Pictures **p. 37** Mary Evans Picture Library **p. 38** Peter Newark's American Pictures **p. 39** Mary Evans Picture Library **p. 40** The Bridgeman Art Library **p. 41** The Bridgeman Art Library **p. 42** (top) The Bridgeman Art Library (bottom) Mary Evans Picture Library **p. 43** the art archive **p. 44** Mary Evans Picture Library **p. 45** The Bridgeman Art Library **p. 47** (top) The Bridgeman Art Library (bottom) The Bridgeman Art Library **p. 48** Mary Evans Picture Library **p. 49** (top) Mary Evans Picture Library (bottom) Mary Evans Picture Library **p. 50** The Bridgeman Art Library **p. 51** (top) Peter Newark's American Pictures (bottom) the art archive **p. 52** Mary Evans Picture Library **p. 53** Mary Evans Picture Library **p. 54** the art archive **p. 55** (top) Mary Evans Picture Library (bottom) The Bridgeman Art Library **p. 56** Mary Evans Picture Library **p. 57** (top) Mary Evans Picture Library (bottom) Peter Newark's American Pictures **p. 58** The Bridgeman Art Library **p. 60** Mary Evans Picture Library **p. 61** (top) Mary Evans Picture Library (bottom) The Bridgeman Art Library **p. 62** The Bridgeman Art Library **p. 63** (top) Peter Newark's American Pictures (bottom) The Bridgeman Art Library **p. 64** Mary Evans Picture Library **p. 65** (top) Peter Newark's American Pictures (bottom) Corbis **p. 67** (top) Topham Picturepoint (bottom) Mary Evans Picture Library **p. 68** Topham Picturepoint **p. 69** Mary Evans Picture Library **p. 70** Topham Picturepoint **p. 71** Topham Picturepoint **p. 72** Mary Evans Picture Library

CONTENTS

THE ORIGINS OF SLAVERY

This basalt stone tablet, dating from nearly 4,000 years ago, is inscribed with Hammurabi, the King of Babylon's code of law. Among its 300 laws, the code states that helping a slave to escape was to be punished by a death sentence; slaves who escaped but were recaptured could be executed.

Slavery in the Ancient World

Slavery is the enforced servitude of people to another person or group. A slave is regarded as someone's property through birth, purchase, or capture. As a social and economic institution, slavery appears to have originated when humans abandoned hunting and gathering in favor of subsistence farming. Among early civilizations, references to slavery are recorded in the Babylonian code of Hammurabi and in the Bible. Forms of slavery were known in ancient China, and slave labor was a fact of life in ancient Greece and Rome, where slaves worked on large estates and as domestic servants in towns and cities. Often, slaves were prisoners of war, the children of slave parents, children sold into slavery by free parents, or criminals condemned to servitude.

Slavery in Asia and Africa

Numerous types of servitude developed throughout the world covering a range of purposes, from solving a chronic labor shortage to meeting the demand for victims of ritual sacrifice. Besides working as agricultural laborers and servants, some slaves were able to exercise considerable power as stewards who managed large estates in China. Other slaves were captured as young boys in southern Europe and forcibly converted to Islam, before being given a rigorous military training by their African or Middle Eastern owners. These warriors were able to achieve high rank in the armies of some Islamic countries. Female slaves were sometimes more highly prized than males in some parts of Africa and the Middle East, since they often served as wives and concubines. In Africa, a trans-Saharan trade in captives for sale existed before, during, and after the period of the transatlantic slave trade.

Slavery in Europe

Following the decline of the Roman Empire in the west, a prominent feature of European society was the large number of agricultural slaves known as serfs. These

slaves were bound by law to the land where they worked. Serfdom was a common form of agricultural labor and persisted until at least the 19th century in some parts of Europe. In areas of France, elements of serfdom survived until the French Revolution at the end of the 18th century, when nobles renounced their feudal rights. Another form of forced labor or servitude in modern Europe was the custom of young apprentices or servants signing a contract that bound them to a master for a number of years in return for food, shelter, and possibly, learning a trade.

Like so many slaves in the New World, Russian serfs were not given their freedom until the second half of the 19th century.

Slavery in the New World

Following the defeat of the Moors in Spain and Portugal in the 15th century, captured Muslims were enslaved by the victorious Christians. Soon, these prisoners of war were joined by slaves imported from Africa. A regular trade in slaves was established between the Guinea coast of Africa and the Iberian peninsula. Colonists cultivating sugar cane on Atlantic islands, such as Madeira and the Canaries, relied on a mixture of slave and free labor. In the 16th century, African slaves were also transported to colonies in the Americas, marking the beginning of a transatlantic slave trade that would transform the history of West Africa, and play a huge part in the social and economic development of Western Europe and the Americas.

African captives landing at Jamestown, Virginia, in 1619.

7

PART I: DEVELOPMENT OF THE
TRANSATLANTIC SLAVE TRADE

EUROPE AND THE SLAVE TRADE

American Colonies

The transatlantic slave trade developed in the 16th century, as European states established colonies in South and Central America. In the last decade of the 15th century, following the discoveries of Christopher Columbus in the New World, the Spanish established colonies in the eastern half of Hispaniola (now the Dominican Republic), Cuba, other islands in the Caribbean, and in South America. In 1500 Portugal took possession of Brazil, which was to become their largest and most important colony in the Americas.

Colonization continued early in the 17th century with the English taking over Barbados, Jamaica, and several other Caribbean islands, while the French settled in Guadeloupe and Martinique. In order to exploit the economic potential of these colonies, the European colonial powers needed an extensive supply of labor. For example, where conditions were favorable, the Spanish and Portuguese had started to grow sugarcane to be processed and shipped back to Europe.

Plantations were set up in Brazil, Mexico, Paraguay, the Pacific coast of South America, and islands in the Caribbean. European colonizers had also discovered that crops such as rice, citrus fruits, olives, and tobacco grew well in these new colonies. Native inhabitants were pressed into service as forced labor, but many died of overwork, disease, and hunger, or simply ran off into the forests. Free labor from Europe chose to

The harvesting and processing of sugarcane to produce sugar in its many forms became the focus of economic life on many Caribbean islands, such as Antigua.

live in urban areas where they were employed as craftsmen and artisans, or took to self-employment in agriculture because fertile land was abundant. The Spanish and Portuguese therefore decided to import slave labor from the Atlantic islands and mainland Africa to work on sugar plantations, coffee and cocoa estates, or in gold and silver mines.

European Consumers

Population growth and economic change had led to improved standards of living in European towns and cities. Consumer demand grew quickly for plantation produce such as sugar, tobacco, coffee, and cocoa. In response, colonists in the Americas enlarged their estates and purchased slave labor from Africa to increase the production of crops that commanded a high price from European traders. Thus, growing consumer demand for colonial produce in European markets encouraged colonists to purchase more slaves to meet that demand.

The Spanish and Portuguese shipped huge numbers of African slaves across the Atlantic to work in colonies such as Cuba and Brazil. Next, the Dutch took advantage of their enormous banking and shipping resources to become financiers of the burgeoning slave trade. They supplied many of the slave ships required to transport tens of thousands of Africans to servitude in the New World.

The *Southall* frigate was one of many European vessels trading on the coast of West Africa in the 17th century. Its crew would have found African traders eager to obtain European goods in exchange for captives.

French Colonies

Production in the French colonies, however, did not occur until the last quarter of the 18th century, with the most dramatic development taking place in the colony of Saint-Domingue (now Haiti). From 1760, this French colony's sugar production expanded dramatically, and the colonists set about increasing their production of coffee and cotton by taking advantage of the terrain and soil of their island. The result of this expansion in plantation production was a huge increase in the number of slaves employed in the colony, and the proportion of African-born slaves within the total population of Saint-Domingue was greater than that of any other large colony in the Americas.

Triangular Trade

European governments were attracted to the economic benefits of possessing colonies in the New World, and sought to exploit the commercial advantages of using slave labor. Slavery and the trade in slaves proved to be major factors in the economic development of Europe's colonial powers. A lucrative long-distance transatlantic slave trade developed as a complex network of commercial enterprises. Most, however, saw the trade process as essentially triangular. First, European goods such as alcohol, firearms, and textiles were shipped from Europe to be traded for slaves in West Africa. Second, the slaves would then be shipped to South America or the Caribbean where they would be traded for staples such as sugar, tobacco, and later, raw cotton. Third, these products of the American colonies were exported to Europe and sold for large profits. In reality, the trade process was much more complex than this. For example, in the 18th century, two out of every five slave ships sailed to and from ports in the Americas.

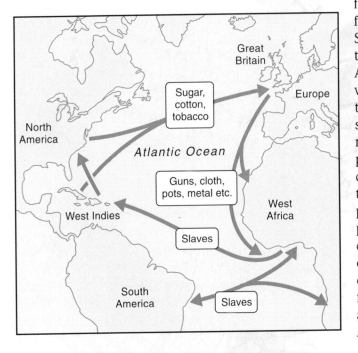

A map showing the 18th-century triangular transatlantic trade.

Extent of the Trade

During the 18th century, European merchants controlled the transatlantic slave trade along a 1,000-mile stretch of the West African coast. At least ten million African captives were transported across the Atlantic between 1500 and the end of the 19th century. By the end of the 18th century, two African captives had crossed the Atlantic for every European colonist who had sailed to the Americas. Half of those Africans were transported in the 18th century, and most were carried on Portuguese, British, or French vessels, with assistance from Spanish, Dutch, Danish, and Swedish ships. A significant proportion of the Portuguese and British ships sailed from colonies in the Americas. Some

In the late 17th century, European slave traders could spend months sailing up and down the African coast. They would row ashore at regular intervals to meet chiefs and traders who could supply them with captives to fill their holds before they set off on the Middle Passage.

Commerce.

Documents, like this list of slaves exported from Cameroon at the end of the 18th century, are often the only clue to the ethnic origin of the millions of captives who were transported to the New World.

British slave traders operated out of ports in New England and Barbados. They supplied colonies in the Caribbean and on the mainland of North and South America, while Portuguese traders sailed from Bahia in Brazil and supplied their own colonies. In total, Brazil and the Caribbean islands bought 90 percent of the African captives who survived the journey, known as the Middle Passage, from West Africa to the West Indies.

During the 18th century, slaves accounted for about 70 percent of the total population of the Caribbean region, and in those European colonies where sugarcane was the main crop, the slave population could account for nearly 90 percent of the total population. The size of the slave population in Europe's American colonies reached its peak at the end of the 18th century, although the number of slaves in the former European colonies of Brazil and the United States of America continued to grow until the 1840s and 1850s, respectively.

Slave caravans were crossing North Africa long before the Europeans took an interest in the trade. European slave traders were able to take advantage of existing trade routes and African merchants' contacts and expertise.

Captives were transported long distances to reach the markets and trading centers on the west coast of Africa.

Effects in Africa

Before the transatlantic slave trade developed, Europeans bought African slaves who had been transported by slave traders across the Sahara region to North Africa. As the number of captives crossing the Atlantic Ocean grew, trade between Africans and Europeans stimulated change and growth in the economy of West Africa.

African farming adapted by growing crops used to provision the slave ships. The areas that supplied agricultural produce for the transatlantic trade were not always the same as those that provided slaves. Captives were taken from almost the whole area of West Africa, but crops were supplied from areas with reliable routes to the trading stations on the coast. The reason for this was the high cost of transportation in West Africa. Marching captives to the coast presented few problems, but agricultural produce had to be transported, either by water or on porters' heads. Since the price of a single captive was roughly equivalent to that of a ton of palm oil (which would require about 60 porters to carry it any distance), it was not profitable to produce palm oil or any other agricultural produce for export unless it was grown close to the coast or a navigable river.

Slave Trading Centers in Africa

On the coast of West Africa, as many as 75 percent of African captives embarked from Luanda, the Zaire or Congo River, the Niger Delta, and the Bight of Benin. Coastal states developed transportation and trading networks that were able to supply small trading centers or larger trading forts with captives from the interior. European slave traders expected supplies to be regular and reliable. At some trading sites, African merchants developed road and river networks from the interior to the coast. One British slave trader, Thomas Clarkson, described in 1789 how he accompanied African traders as their fleet of canoes:

called at villages as we passed, and purchased our slaves fairly; but in the night they made several excursions on the banks of the river ...broke into the villages...and seized men, women, and children.

Over time, the focus of the slave trade moved south, and West Central Africa was the center of the trade in its final decades. When the British attempted to enforce a ban on the transatlantic slave trade in the early 19th century, traders south of the equator continued to supply Brazil and Cuba from Angola and Mozambique. As colonies developed and required more forced labor, some regions of Africa supplied the bulk of slaves shipped to particular colonies.

The Portuguese colony of Brazil received most of its slaves from Angola and the Bight of Benin, also known as the Slave Coast. The French colony of Saint-Domingue took a large proportion of its captives from the Bight of Benin, too. The British colonies were supplied with captives from a wide range of regions, but the Bight of Biafra, the Gold Coast, and Angola were Great Britain's main sources of slaves in the second half of the 18th century. The island of Cuba was unique in that the Spanish government allowed the colony to receive slave shipments from most European merchants and, as a result, no single African region supplied more than one-third of Cuba's slaves.

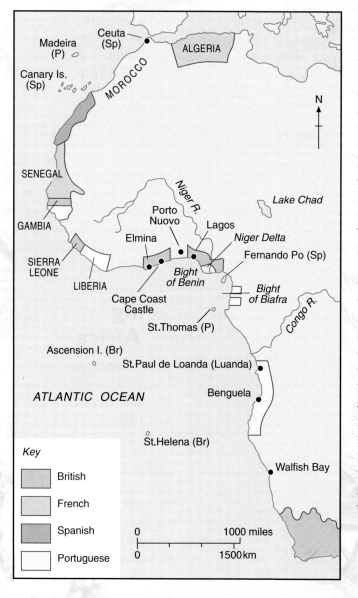

A map of West Africa showing the location of the chief slave-trading regions.

13

European Trade with Africa

European traders tried to cheat the Africans at every turn. Alcohol was diluted with water, gunpowder barrels had false bottoms, and pieces were cut out of rolls of cloth. Chiefs and kings stopped ruling by traditional laws and customs and became greedy tyrants, taking advice from the slave traders' ruthless European agents. In the 16th century, King Affonso of the Congo complained to the Portuguese that:

so great is the corruption and lawlessness that our country is being completely depopulated.

The vast majority of African children who were abducted by raiders would be unable to trace their parents or return to their home villages.

Tribal wars became more common, encouraged by the profits that could be made from the slave trade. Law and justice were corrupted as more and more crimes, no matter how small, were punished by enslavement. Thousands of villages were gradually deserted as a result of wars or raids to capture slaves.

Africans Supply Slaves

Some African states, which had enslaved captives for many years, enslaved yet more people when the transatlantic slave trade developed. From the late 17th century, Ashanti (Asante) traded slaves and captives for European goods, such as cloth, alcohol, and guns. It used these resources to make itself more powerful, and to start wars against its neighbors in order to acquire more captives. Another African kingdom that took advantage of the transatlantic slave trade was Dahomey. In the 18th century, the kings of Dahomey organized raids into neighboring lands largely to capture prisoners to sell to European traders. On a smaller scale, other kingdoms took part in the slave trade, venturing far inland to take captives to sell to Europeans. In these coastal areas, native crafts died out, unable to compete with the cheap European goods mass produced in factories.

This image of the King of Dahomey gives us some idea of the power and prestige of those African rulers who profited from the trade in African captives.

Profits of Slave Labor

The transatlantic trade in human cargo, and the crops that slave labor produced, financed the building of new harbors and the construction of new shipyards in the British Isles. This led to increased orders for goods produced for export to Africa and the American colonies. In the second half of the 18th century, Great Britain's major seaports made huge profits from transatlantic trade.

Slaves produced about 75 percent of the total value of exports from the Americas traded in the Atlantic area in the 17th and 18th centuries. By the end of the 18th century, British industries producing for export markets were growing faster than those producing mainly for the domestic market. Liverpool merchants sent a petition to Parliament in 1788 claiming that abolition of the slave trade would:

ruin the property of the English merchants in the West Indies, diminish the public revenue, and impair [weaken] the maritime strength of Great Britain.

Race Relations

Ethnic and religious differences between the European slave owners and their African slaves helped to permit master–slave relationships in the minds of the Europeans and distinguish between those who could be forcibly enslaved and those who could not. Modern European slavery in the colonial era was characterized by its ethnic composition. Most slaves were African by birth, or the descendants of Africans who had been transported to European colonies in North and South America. Most slave owners were Europeans or their descendants.

Diverse conditions and traditions fostered variations between societies in the European colonies, in terms of both slavery and race relations, but slavery in Europe's American colonies was based on an unequal relationship between Europeans and non-Europeans. This inequality has had repercussions for race relations in the European and American world ever since.

In the 18th century, the ownership of slaves in Great Britain's American colonies not only provided a large labor force on plantations, but was a mark of wealth and prestige.

European Civilization and Slavery

From ancient times, European states had exploited slave labor. Ancient attitudes toward Europeans who were enslaved were similar to those faced by African captives in the modern era. The Greek soldier Xenophon wrote a manual for slave owners, giving advice on how to select suitable slaves for employment on a large estate. In particular, he emphasized the qualities of intelligence, energy, loyalty, and experience necessary for any slave in a position of responsibility.

The philosopher Plato, writing 2,500 years ago, believed that Greeks should not be enslaved by Greeks, but he did not conclude that slavery was unjust. Instead, he wrote that slavery should be restricted to foreigners or "barbarians," and that the status of slave could be inherited from parents. At that stage in European civilization, the enslaved were considered inferior to their owners. The philosopher Aristotle, a pupil of Plato, wrote:

Xenophon's book on how to handle slaves reminds us that early Europeans took slavery for granted.

From the hour of their birth some are marked out for subjection, others for rule.

Aristotle went so far as to suggest that it was the duty of superior Greeks to enslave inferior barbarians, in order that both groups could fulfill their true functions and mutually benefit.

The brutal treatment of captives and the enslavement of prisoners came together in the use of slave gladiators in the arenas of the Roman Empire.

Ancient Rome

The Roman Empire swallowed up most of southern and western Europe, and most of North Africa. Slaves were imperial victims whose lives were held cheap by ruthless rulers who enjoyed absolute power over their conquests. For centuries, the citizens of the Roman Empire demanded the deaths of thousands of slave gladiators each year for their entertainment, and tolerated the branding, burning, beating, and mutilation of slaves by owners who believed that these people were property, not human beings with civil rights. Roman ideas about government and society continued to influence European civilization when the transatlantic slave trade developed.

Exploration and Oppression

The Portuguese and Spanish explorers and settlers who set sail for the Americas across the Atlantic in the 1490s took for granted their right to enslave enemies and exploit forced labor. Mistakenly believing that they were exploring the Indies in Southeast Asia, the explorers called the people who lived on these islands Indians. A more serious error was the failure of these explorers to appreciate the differences between their own European culture and beliefs, and those of the many peoples whom they encountered. The simple technology, hospitality, and generosity of so many native peoples were mistaken for signs of weakness, and the superiority of European civilization and their weapons was assumed at all times. Columbus described the inhabitants of the island that he named Hispaniola as being kind, peaceful, and generous, but he noted in his journal:

With fifty men they could all be subjected and made to do all that I wished.

An artist's impression of Peruvians from Lima, drawn about 1700. Three centuries later, archaeologists are still uncovering evidence of the achievements of the civilizations that inhabited the Americas before the arrival of Europeans in the 15th and 16th centuries.

European Violence

Contact between Europe and the New World led to death and misery on a huge scale. Within fifty years of Columbus's setting foot on the island, it is estimated that the native population of Hispaniola fell from approximately 300,000 to less than 1,000, due to disease, war, and the mistreatment of captives. From the outset, servitude in the Americas would be characterized by cruelty and violence toward non-Europeans. By 1600, nearly one million African captives had been transported across the Atlantic. Most of these victims would meet a fate similar to that of the people they were replacing. The development of Europe's transatlantic trade demanded a high price from captives exploited by traders, who paid little attention to the humanity of their victims.

Plantation records, government files, colonists' diaries and letters, and the accounts left by freed men and women describe the brutality that slave ownership encouraged and allowed.

THE MIDDLE PASSAGE

Coastal Trade

This image of two merchants on an island off Senegal is a reminder of how European slave traders developed close links with the Africans who supplied captives for the Middle Passage.

In Africa, most of the trade in captives was carried out at markets in the small trading factories or larger stone forts along the Atlantic coast. Where there were no proper harbor facilities, slave ships would sail up and down the coast collecting batches of captives who were ferried to the ships in small boats and canoes. Ships' captains had to inspect the captives to assess whether or not they would survive the voyage and make a good price in the slave markets of the Americas. Some captains could spend four or five months plying their trade along the African coast until they had enough slaves to fill their holds.

The Middle Passage

The death rate among sailors involved in trade with Africa was very high. Since a significant proportion of the crew was likely to die from disease before they reached the Americas, crew levels could fall to dangerous levels. Slave ship captains had to be prepared to face storms and slave rebellions during what was known as the Middle Passage, and they needed as large a crew as possible to reach the other side of the Atlantic Ocean.

Two iron slave collars from around 1790. Archaeologists have found collars and chains small enough to fit children or small adults.

Adult females made up about 25 percent of the African captives who were forced into slavery in the Americas. For much of the 18th century, this ratio was largely determined by African supply conditions. Most captives were male prisoners of war, placing female slaves in much higher demand than males in Africa's local domestic slave trade.

Children of both sexes made up roughly ten percent of the slaves carried on the Middle Passage. Their numbers declined rapidly due to physical and sexual abuse aboard the vessels, and the ravages of smallpox, measles, and other diseases also contributed to the high mortality rate among the younger captives. Because there were so few female slaves in relation to males, the slave populations in most European colonies in the New World failed to reproduce their numbers.

Slave vessels setting sail on the Middle Passage from West African trading centers on the Gambia, Senegal, and Sierra Leone rivers could take four to six weeks to complete the voyage. The passage could take several months from regions farther east such as the Bight of Benin. Early in the history of the transatlantic slave trade, almost 20 percent of African captives died during the Middle Passage. By the late 18th century, less than ten percent of slaves died crossing the Atlantic, mainly due to improvements in hygiene and sanitation aboard the ships.

Bills of Exchange

Slave ship captains and colonial merchants sold slaves to plantation owners in return for what were known as bills of exchange. These bills could be exchanged for cargoes of plantation produce on the return trip, but most slave vessels were not large enough to transport more than a fraction of the colonies' produce back to Europe. Instead, most colonial produce was carried on larger vessels known to the British as "West Indiamen." The smaller slave-carrying vessels did not play a significant part in the final leg of the triangular trade.

A Dutch ship landing captives at Jamestown, Virginia, in 1619. Most African captives initially landed in the Caribbean and South America in the 17th and 18th centuries. Captives were carried in ships from most major European trading nations.

Slave Ships

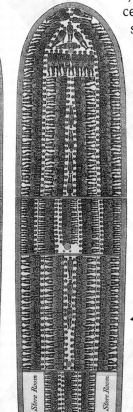

Slave ships were small by modern standards, although they grew in size between the 17th and 19th centuries—from about 100 to 300 tons. Slave ships were rigged for speed and most carried between 200 and 300 captives. Modern diagrams of slave ships show how the captives were stacked below decks for the voyage. Often there were two levels, one above the other, on either side of the ship. Adult male captives had their right foot shackled to the left foot of the person on their right, and their left foot shackled to the right foot of the person on their left. The human cargo had little or no head room, making it impossible for them to sit up. Because they were chained, they found it difficult to change position. A doctor in 1790 noted that on overcrowded ships the captives:

complained of heat and want of air. Confinement in this situation was so injurious that he has known them to go down apparently in good health at night and found dead in the morning.

Women and children were not chained as a rule, but were liable to face physical and sexual abuse from sailors throughout the voyage.

Deck plans for the slave ship *Brookes*, which sailed out of Liverpool, England, at the end of the 18th century. Each male captive was allowed less than a 6-foot by 16-inch area of space, so that the vessel could pack in 450 slaves.

Each day, when the weather permitted, some captives were taken on deck to exercise. Exercise, or "dancing," was thought to prevent outbreaks of disease among the captives. When the sea was rough or the weather was inclement, the captives were kept below deck for long periods, and the sick and healthy, living and dead, or dying, remained chained together for days on end. Most ships carried a medical assistant or doctor, but outbreaks of dysentery were common due to filthy conditions and lack of clean drinking water.

Captive Resistance

Many African captives on the Middle Passage committed suicide. Some took the opportunity when exercising above deck to jump overboard and drown. Some appeared to lose the will to live and died from what was called "fixed melancholy." These captives would refuse

In fair weather, small groups of captives were brought up onto the main deck to dance during the voyage. This kept them fit and healthy so they would fetch a good price when they reached the slave markets in the Americas.

A contemporary illustration showing the death of Captain Ferrer of the *Amistad*, when the captives seized control of the ship. The future of the captives aboard the *Amistad* led to a legal battle in the U.S. courts between the ship's owners and abolitionists.

to eat. To discourage this form of resistance, crews beat or tortured them with thumbscrews. If this did not work, sailors force-fed the captives. Crews were known to use chisels to break the teeth of captives who resisted being force-fed. The slave traders were worried that if one captive refused to eat, others would follow suit and a large number of valuable Africans would die.

Slave Rebellions

Europeans were always on guard against captives attempting to take control of the ship by killing the crew. One slave trader, John Newton, noted in his journal in 1753:

I was at first continually alarmed with the slaves' almost desperate attempts to make attacks upon us.

Rebellions were most likely to occur when ships were off the African coast, before they set sail across the Atlantic. Most uprisings were put down ruthlessly by the European crews, but there were a few occasions when captives took control of the vessel on which they had been held captive. In 1742 the British vessel *Mary* was driven ashore on the Gambia River by the local people, and the captives on board managed to kill most of the crew before escaping. However, the success of this group of captives was the exception rather than the rule.

The sale of African captives could take place aboard the slave ship, on a beach, or in a large seaport. This 17th-century Dutch auction of African slaves took place ashore in New Amsterdam (later New York).

This branding iron was used to mark and identify slaves on arrival.

Preparations for Sale

Having completed the voyage across the Atlantic, slave traders were determined to present their African captives to potential purchasers in the best possible condition. The captives who had survived the voyage were washed and fed for several days. Males were shaved and older captives had their gray hair dyed to make it more difficult to guess their age. Often, their skin was rubbed with palm oil to give their bodies a healthy sheen. Older or less healthy individuals might not attract any bids from colonists or their agents. They could be taken on to other islands where they could be put up for sale until they attracted a buyer, but sometimes these "refuse" slaves were left to die of neglect, unattended at the wharf of the port where they had disembarked.

Slave Sales

The captives could be sold aboard the ship soon after it arrived, or at a public auction ashore. In some ports the captains of slave ships handed their human cargo over to agents for the vessels' owners. These agents inspected the captives as if they were livestock, checking limbs and teeth for defects, before advertising the place and time of the slave sale. Captives would be listed for sale by sex, approximate age, and sometimes provenance or geographic origin, if known.

In Spanish and Portuguese colonies, newly arrived slaves would be branded with a red hot iron to indicate that they had been imported legally.

In the Caribbean, captives were often sold through a "scramble" when prospective purchasers and their associates ran forward and claimed those captives whom they wanted to buy at an agreed price.

Despite attempts to present new arrivals as fit and healthy, many colonists avoided buying captives who had just completed the Middle Passage since they could be carrying infectious diseases that threatened the existing slave population. Some colonists were not

When they were sold, captives would be separated from their fellow victims who had accompanied them on the Middle Passage, and they would be given a European name in place of their African name.

prepared to train recently arrived captives, who had to be acclimatized to their new environment and taught the skills of plantation laborers. Although some colonists were prepared to wait until newly purchased slaves had recovered from the effects of the Atlantic crossing, many put new arrivals to work at once, especially if they were purchased at harvest time when labor was in short supply.

Many African captives were bought in Barbados and the Leeward Islands and then shipped to the North American mainland, where they were sold either to colonists or to other traders who sold them to slave owners in the interior of the colonies. Charleston in South Carolina was the main port of direct entry for slaves in North America during the 18th century. Here, ships carrying captives had to wait outside the port at Sullivan Island for ten days. If the slaves aboard any ship turned out to be suffering from smallpox, the ship would be quarantined for at least four weeks.

A poster advertising a slave auction of captives from Sierra Leone in Charleston, South Carolina, in 1769.

Charlestown, July 24th, 1769.

TO BE SOLD,

On THURSDAY the third Day of AUGUST next,

A CARGO

OF

NINETY-FOUR

PRIME, HEALTHY

NEGROES,

CONSISTING OF

Thirty-nine MEN, Fifteen BOYS, Twenty-four WOMEN, and Sixteen GIRLS.

JUST ARRIVED,

In the Brigantine DEMBIA, Francis Bare, Master, from SIERRA-LEON, by

DAVID & JOHN DEAS.

The European Enlightenment

The term *Enlightenment* refers to the changes in attitudes and beliefs that began in Europe around 300 years ago. European scientists, philosophers, and political commentators in the 18th century, many known as *philosophes*, were united in the belief that rational, critical study and analysis should be applied in all matters. Many criticized political, social, and economic practices that appeared to be irrational, such as superstitious religion or tyrannical rule. They argued that the rational or reasoned foundation of government should be the welfare or well-being of the governed, who had "natural rights" such as the right to fight against tyranny. These ideas developed at a time when Europeans were reaping the benefits of employing millions of slaves in the Americas. Rousseau, in his *Social Contract* (1762), wrote:

Man was born free, but everywhere he is in chains.

Revolutionary Ideals

At the time of the American Revolution, slavery and the slave trade remained key elements of economic prosperity in a large number of the colonies, which were united in their fight against British rule. In their Declaration of Independence, the American colonists included the enlightened phrase:

Thomas Jefferson (1743–1826), third president of the United States, was a founding father of the U.S. and a slave owner.

All men are created equal.

In the draft of this Declaration, Thomas Jefferson, a slave owner, had condemned the slave trade. However, it is clear that he believed that Africans were beings inferior to Europeans, and he was not prepared to give up his property or lose political influence through active opposition to slavery. The leaders of the American Revolution who were influenced by the ideas of the 18th-century Enlightenment were not social revolutionaries. When the federal Constitution of the United States was drafted in 1787, the legal status of slavery in the southern states, where about 90 percent of American slaves lived, was strengthened.

In the 1790s, the French revolutionaries set out the principles of their revolution in a Declaration of the Rights of Man and of the Citizen that stated:

Men are born free and remain free and equal in their rights.

Despite the lofty ideals of the Enlightenment, political intrigue and economic self-interest meant that slavery and the slave trade would remain facts of life for too many people in the French empire. In 1794 the French abolished slavery in their colonies and accepted all colonial males as full citizens, only to have Napoleon Bonaparte restore colonial slavery in 1802.

Humanitarian Ideals

Influenced by the ideals of the Enlightenment, some Europeans embarked on crusades against colonial slavery rather than against other forms of servitude and forced labor closer to home. From the beginning, campaigns against slavery exhibited a form of paternalism toward Africans and their descendants in European colonies. This approach was encouraged by real or imagined images of exotic, but apparently primitive, societies and cultures in Africa and the Americas, which gave some credibility to a simplistic moral crusade on behalf of Africans. Even those who opposed slavery were guilty of assuming that slaves were somehow inferior to free Europeans.

A public execution at Tyburn in London. A death sentence was common for most serious, as well as many less serious, crimes in 18th- and 19th-century Europe. How far did humanitarian ideals really extend at this time?

SLAVE LIFE IN THE AMERICAS

Slave Imports

More than 90 percent of the slaves who were transported across the Atlantic were imported by European colonies on the South American mainland and the Caribbean islands. Conditions in these colonies were so harsh that slave deaths exceeded slave births. Climate, tropical diseases, and exhausting labor on sugar plantations contributed to the failure of the slave populations in these colonies to achieve natural population growth. Slave owners continued to import large numbers of African slaves until the trade was abolished. Despite the existence of an illegal slave trade well into the 19th century, the slave population continued to decline.

The Sugar Trade

Several European nations took advantage of the trading opportunities made possible by establishing colonies in the Americas. By the middle of the 18th century, most

This illustration of sugar manufacture in the Antilles in 1726 is evidence of the labor-intensive production methods that were necessary in order to export sugar to Europe.

European colonies in the region were committed to exporting sugar. Five British islands in the Caribbean produced cotton, timber, fish, livestock, and salt, but 14 British colonies concentrated on sugar production. By 1789 the French island of Saint-Domingue was the single largest sugar-producing colony in the Americas. The Dutch colony of Suriname on the mainland of South America imported African slaves to work on its plantations, and around one quarter of the population of the Danish island of Saint Thomas were slaves employed on sugar plantations. The Swedish colony of Saint Barthelemy was an exception in that its slaves were restricted to working as domestic servants or as farm laborers producing food for consumption on the island.

On sugar plantations, slaves worked under the gang system and were assigned tasks and roles according to color of skin, place of birth, gender, state of health, age, and skills. Slaves who were considered by their European owners to have lighter skin, and had been born in the Americas, were preferred for domestic service. Male and female slaves worked in the fields, and there was little or no difference in the types of field work carried out by either sex. Men and women were expected to tackle the most arduous tasks in the fields and sugar factories. An 18th-century Swiss visitor to Saint-Domingue described how he saw:

about a hundred men and women of different ages, all occupied in digging ditches in a cane-field, the majority of them naked or covered in rags.

Slaves planting sugarcane in Antigua in 1823. How would the working day of a plantation slave differ from the experience of a free laborer employed in similar activities?

Field Labor on Plantations

At harvest time, slaves on sugar plantations had to work shifts of 18 to 24 hours for five or six months at a time, since the sugarcane had to be processed without interruption. Field labor on sugar plantations was divided into three gangs. The first gang consisted of the fittest and healthiest slaves of both sexes who were experts in preparing the soil for cultivation, digging cane holes, planting and fertilizing the canes, burning and cutting the sugarcane at harvest time, and performing manual labor in the sugar mills. They worked under the supervision of European overseers and male slave drivers.

The second gang was supervised by a male slave driver and was made up of less fit males and females, pregnant or nursing females, and slaves recently arrived from Africa. They performed a variety of less physically demanding tasks, including weeding crops, carrying manure to the cane fields, and feeding crushed cane stalks into the sugar factory furnaces. The third gang consisted of children up to the age of 12 or 13 who were supervised by a mature female slave, and this gang looked after the plantation's livestock.

Slaves employed in processing sugarcane developed considerable expertise and a range of skills that were valued by their owners. However, paying wages to an army of workers would have made these methods uneconomic.

On many Caribbean islands, and to a lesser extent in Brazil, a significant number of slaves were able to achieve a level of economic independence by cultivating crops on plots of land granted by their masters. These slaves could sell their surplus and acquire their own property and possessions.

Slave Emancipation

Despite attempts to bring the transatlantic slave trade to an end, African captives continued to be transported to the Americas for much of the 19th century, until slavery was abolished throughout South America and the Caribbean. A revolution in Saint-Domingue between 1791 and 1804 won independence for the French colony and freed its slaves. The colony's slaves had marched to the words of a song that stated:

Better to die than go on being a slave.

Former slaves celebrating their emancipation in Barbados, in August 1834. Similar scenes were repeated throughout the Americas in the 19th century by millions of freed laborers.

Sweden had handed back its only Caribbean colony to the French, long before slavery was abolished in the British Empire in 1834. All slaves were freed in the French and Danish colonies by 1848, and the Dutch abolished slavery in their colonies in 1863. Slavery came to an end in the Spanish Caribbean between 1870 and 1886, but Brazilian slaves were not emancipated until 1888.

Slavery remained profitable and therefore viable in both Brazil and Cuba until the 1870s, despite attempts by the Portuguese and Spanish governments to end the use of forced labor in both colonies. In the end, it would be political and technological change that would emancipate these slaves. In the case of Cuba, a more liberal regime in Spain and pro-independence rebels in the colony both declared their support for emancipation. Once the powerful plantation owners had built large, modern sugar mills, served by a network of railway lines, Cuban slaves were free to become wage laborers employed on a seasonal basis. Direct action by free citizens, plus the introduction of more efficient machinery in sugar mills, ended slavery in Brazil in the late 1880s.

As forced labor, most slaves employed in the fields had to be compelled to work by their owners and drivers. Beatings and whippings, or the threat of them, were a fact of life for most field hands.

Slavery in North America

Farmers in the North American colonies discovered that huge profits could be made from growing and exporting crops such as tobacco and cotton to Europe. Where fertile land was plentiful, but labor was in short supply, the most practical solution was the use of forced or slave labor. Some of the Native-American inhabitants of the colonies had been enslaved, but several factors prevented the development of large-scale slavery in this population, including the fact that so many of them had died in epidemics that swept through local communities due to a lack of immunity to diseases such as smallpox and measles. Also, the European colonists preferred to kill or drive away local inhabitants, rather than consider them as agricultural labor.

From Indenture to Slavery

In the first half of the 17th century, the solution to the colonists' labor shortage was the employment of indentured or bond servants. Indentured servitude meant that Europeans unable to afford to pay for their own passage to the American colonies could sell their labor to colonists for an agreed number of years, in exchange for their transportation to America. Although criminals were transported to the American colonies, most bond servants were young males from poor backgrounds, attempting to escape from poverty, hunger, unemployment, or military service. Children often served seven or more years, but most adults served four or five years of indentured service. Discipline could be brutal and the corporal punishment of runaways was a common practice.

From 1650 to 1700, although the free population of some colonies doubled or tripled, the number of indentured servants did not keep pace with the demand for farm labor. In Europe, higher wages and improved employment opportunities at home meant that fewer people were attracted to indentured servitude in North America. Colonial landowners who were unable to obtain a constant supply of European servants decided to use African slaves instead. Unlike indentured servitude, slavery was for life, and it was common for female slaves to pass their status on to their children, even if a child's father was a European. The African-American writer W. E. B. DuBois wrote:

 We cannot forget that America was built on Africa....America became through African labor the center of the sugar empire and the cotton kingdom.

American-born Slaves

Out of the ten to eleven million Africans who crossed the Atlantic on the Middle Passage, only 6 percent of that total were taken to the British colonies in North America. In the 18th century, and in sharp contrast to the Caribbean and South America, the slave population of North America experienced a natural population growth. By the 1760s the number of American-born slaves in the colonies overtook the number of African-born slaves. After the United States ban on transatlantic slave trading in 1808, the slave population of the U.S. more than tripled by 1860, from 1.2 million to 4 million, and only a tiny proportion of these slaves were African-born. The fact that so many slaves in North America had been born in the colonies meant that relations between free people and the slave population were profoundly different from those in the Caribbean and South America.

Slavery Declines in the North

Slaves had never formed a significant proportion of the population in the northern colonies of the United States. Climate and soil conditions discouraged plantation farming, and the need for a large labor force did not develop in those colonies. In addition, religious and political principles in the northern states meant that many people were uneasy at the existence of slavery in their communities. The growth of industry and urban communities in the North led to the development of a working class that was hostile to competition from slave labor. It was felt that slave labor would lead to lower wages and less favorable working conditions. As a result, anti-slavery campaigners found it relatively easy to rid the northern states of slavery.

Slavery Develops in the South

Meanwhile, slavery had become entrenched in the South. The booming market in cotton was largely responsible for this development. To meet the growing demand for cotton fiber in British textile factories, plantation owners needed to find a more efficient method of separating cotton seeds from their fiber. In the 1790s Eli Whitney designed a machine that:

The invention of Whitney's cotton gin, or engine, in the 1790s encouraged the rapid growth of cotton production in the Deep South.

would clear the cotton with expedition (speed).

A horse-powered gin could seed 50 times as much cotton as before, in the same amount of time.

When cotton became the United States' main agricultural export in the first half of the 19th century, farmers discovered that large profits could be made from growing cotton on relatively small holdings as well as on larger plantations. This meant that most American slaves did not live on huge estates. In 1860 less than 3 percent of slave owners in the South owned more than 50 slaves, and no more than one out of every thousand slave owners possessed more than 200 slaves. The larger plantations concentrated on growing sugar and rice. Cotton growers tended to live on their land and personally supervised the work of their slaves. Only on larger plantations would professional overseers be employed to carry out the instructions of their employers, usually under the watchful eyes of a resident owner.

African slaves who worked on large Southern sugar plantations did so under the watchful eyes of an overseer.

Life for Southern Slaves

The treatment and condition of slaves in the southern states varied in relation to location, the crop grown, the size of farm or plantation, and the attitude of the slave owner. Nevertheless, it is possible to draw some general conclusions about slavery in the United States. Slavery was overwhelmingly based on agriculture. Most slaves were employed in the production of cotton, rice, tobacco, hemp, wheat, corn, and sugar. Most lived on plantations and farms with between 15 and 50 slaves. Slaves had to endure a great deal. Malnutrition and disease were facts of life. Food, clothing, and shelter were no more than basic for most slaves. Field hands worked hard, for little or no reward. Physical and sexual abuse were common.

Most non-capital offenses against slaves escaped punishment or censure, and only a few whites were tried, convicted, and sentenced for murdering slaves. Besides beatings and mutilation for persistent runaways, the most effective deterrent to slave resistance was the constant threat of being sold and separated from family and friends, since no state's law recognized the existence or validity of slave marriages.

Slave Occupations

Slave occupations tended to be age-specific. Few able-bodied slaves aged 15 to 40 years of age were employed in occupations other than field work. Domestic servants tended to be older children, male and female, or older men and women no longer fit for heavy field work. Few slave owners could afford to have able-bodied slaves who specialized in a particular craft and worked full-time as carpenters or blacksmiths. Most urban slaves were female domestic servants, but some male slaves were employed as dock workers, craftsmen, or factory workers in sugar processing or in sawmills.

Slaves were employed as house servants in the United States, as this 18th-century illustration shows. However, domestic service tended to be restricted to young slaves, or those too old or unfit to work in the fields.

Plantation Labor

On those plantations employing 15 or more slaves, slaves would work in gangs led by a driver chosen from among the male slaves on account of his strength, intelligence, loyalty to his master, and leadership skills. The driver acted as an assistant to the owner or overseer, and personally supervised the work of his slave gang. Slaves employed in field work tended to be described as either plow hands or hoe hands. Plow hands were the fittest able-bodied male and female slaves. Hoe hands were less fit, but were regarded as being more important than the members of the trash gang. This third group was made up of young children and adults incapable of heavy field work. They were employed in tasks such as weeding and yard cleaning. The gang system in the American South was very similar to organization of gang labor on plantations in the Caribbean and South America (see page 28).

Domestic Life

Most slaves lived in wooden cabins or huts, and received a food allowance from their owners. It was common practice for field hands to receive four sets of clothes each year. Male field hands would be given pants and a shirt, and women a dress. These clothes would have been sewn together by slave women, often using cloth that was specially manufactured in American textile mills to be sold to slave owners. Since boots and shoes

These log cabins were home to black field workers in Georgia in the 1860s.

seldom fit properly, most field hands chose to work barefoot.

Many slaves were allowed to grow vegetables and keep chickens on small plots of land. Some were allowed to sell their produce at markets, or barter them for other goods. However, these garden plots were privileges that could be removed at the slave owner's discretion, and slaves were not able to pass on their property to their children or grandchildren.

Urban Slavery

The number of slaves employed in the towns and cities of the South was not significant. In the years immediately before the outbreak of the Civil War in 1861, slaves made up less than 10 percent of the population of the largest cities in the slave-owning states, and no more than 5 percent of the population in smaller towns. Most owners were wary of allowing their slaves to associate with urban slaves, or the free African Americans who tended to live in urban areas rather than in rural regions. One abolitionist noted that:

 a city slave is almost a freeman, compared with a slave on a plantation.

Free African Americans

In the slave-owning states, most free African Americans lived in the upper South, where more than 10 percent of all African Americans were free by 1810. Outside of that area, in the four decades before the outbreak of the Civil War, the number of free African Americans in the South decreased as states passed laws that made it very difficult for owners to free slaves. Free African Americans were encouraged to move north or west, despite the prejudice and discrimination they faced in those regions. In the northern states, freedmen, as they were known, were denied the vote and legal protection, and were often threatened by racist gangs and mobs.

About 30 percent of the free African Americans living in the southern states were described by their neighbors as "people of color." Some were the descendants of unions between French or Spanish slaves and their owners, while others were refugees from the French colony of Saint-Domingue. These free people were called mulattoes in official census documents, but some preferred to call themselves by the less offensive name of Creoles, which was a name also used by the European descendants of French and Spanish colonists. Some African-American Creoles owned slaves. Another group of free "coloreds" consisted of those freed slaves who were the sons and daughters of slave owners, whose parents had chosen to distinguish between them and their other slaves. This custom was common in South America, but much less so in the United States.

Christianity and Slavery

Some African captives were Christians before they arrived in the New World, but the widespread conversion of slaves to Christianity only began in the second half of the 18th century and was accelerated by religious revivals among free Americans during the first half of the 19th century. In the last decades before emancipation, most slaves were Methodists or Baptists, like most of their southern owners. In fact, a significant proportion of slaves attended the same services as their owners, although they worshiped in segregated slave galleries or balconies above the main portion of the church.

Free African Americans formed their own "African"

A religious revival in the U.S. at the beginning of the 19th century led to most slaves being converted to Christianity. This illustration from 1810 suggests that a slave's best hope of freedom would come from heaven … "their day of grace has begun to dawn!"

Baptist or Methodist churches in the late 18th century. In 1787 the Free African Society was formed in Philadelphia by former slaves. Richard Allen, a freed slave, founded the Bethel Church, and this grew into the African Methodist Episcopal Church in 1816. African churches were opened in the cities of the North and in some urban areas of the South. African-American communities, finding themselves excluded from so many organizations by prejudice and discrimination, went on to set up schools and other associations to serve their own communities.

Voodoo

At the same time, pre-Christian beliefs and practices persisted among rural slaves within their own families. Superstition, magic, and folk remedies retained their hold on many illiterate farm laborers, and some slaves used potions, charms, and rituals to ward off evil spirits, treat infections, and frighten enemies. In southern Louisiana, the fusion of African beliefs and elements of Catholicism became known as voodoo, but it was virtually unheard of in the rest of the South.

The Movement Toward Abolition

For most of the 18th century, few Europeans questioned the nature of the slave trade between Africa and the European colonies in the Americas, but toward the end of the century, an increasing number of people began to demand the abolition, the end, of the trade. The first Europeans to openly campaign against the slave trade were the Quakers, or Society of Friends, who declared in 1761 that no person engaged in the slave trade could be a member of their religion.

A significant move against the slave trade in Great Britain was made by Granville Sharp. He tried to use existing laws to fight against the trade. His most dramatic success concerned a runaway slave named Thomas Lewis, who had been kidnapped by his former owner and put on a ship bound for the West Indies. Sharp obtained permission to bring Lewis back to London and to have his case heard in court. The result was that a British court had to admit that it was not clear whether or not it was legal to possess a slave in the British Isles. In 1772 the case of James Somersett came to court. He was a slave who had lived as a free man in London for two years before being recaptured by his former owner. Sharp hired a team of lawyers who persuaded the judge, Lord Mansfield, that Somersett was a free man and that it was illegal to force a runaway slave to leave the British Isles.

Granville Sharp (1735–1813) restraining a sea captain from taking a slave to his ship in 1767. Sharp was a founder of the British Society for the Abolition of the Slave Trade. He concentrated on fighting test cases through British courts to establish legal precedents that would force the trade to come to an end.

The *Zong*

In 1781 horrific events on the slave ship *Zong* focused public attention on the evils of the slave trade. The ship's captain was an experienced slave trader named Collingwood. He had mistaken Jamaica for Saint-Domingue, and after 11 weeks at sea, 7 crew members and over 80 slaves had died. In order to make a profit on the voyage, Collingwood ordered his crew to chain together and throw overboard more than 130 slaves so he could make a claim to the ship's insurers. Ten slaves who witnessed what was happening committed suicide. Following a court case, the ship's owners were able to force the insurers to pay them £30 for each slave whom Collingwood had drowned.

The Campaign Begins

The Society for the Abolition of the Slave Trade was founded in 1787. The Society's main purpose was to campaign for an end to the transatlantic slave trade. The Society decided that to abolish slavery outright would be too expensive if slave owners had to be compensated for the loss of their slaves, and the effects of the abolition of slavery on the colonies and transatlantic trade would hit the British economy too hard. Instead, by abolishing the slave trade they would end the wars in Africa that were fought to enslave thousands of Africans each year, bring to an end the horrors of the Middle Passage, and force slave owners to treat their slaves better, since they would be more difficult to replace.

Leading British abolitionists who campaigned for an end to the slave trade between the British Empire and Africa included Sharp, Macaulay, Wilberforce, Buxton, and Clarkson.

Anti-Slave Trade Arguments

The Society claimed that sugar could be produced more cheaply in British-controlled India using free labor or indentured servants, rather than by relying on slaves in the Americas. It argued that the transatlantic slave trade was holding back the development of British trade with India and the rest of Asia. The Society also produced evidence that hundreds of British seamen involved in the triangular trade died every year, and those who participated in the horrors of the Middle Passage were brutalized by the way that they were forced to treat their human cargoes. In 1798, a poet writing under the name "Guineaman" described his experiences as a sailor on a slave ship with these words:

But some of them were sulky slaves,
And would not take their meat;
So therefore we were forced, by threats
And blows, to make them eat.

Gathering Evidence

Thomas Clarkson had been involved in setting up the Society in 1787 with Granville Sharp. Clarkson set himself the task of collecting evidence that would win support for the abolition of the slave trade. Embarking on his investigations in London, he visited and studied slave ships in the capital, as well as in Bristol and Liverpool. He collected artifacts such as manacles, thumbscrews, and branding irons. Despite intimidation and threats from slave ship captains and owners, Clarkson interviewed over 20,000 sailors and collected a mountain of evidence about the horrific conditions aboard slave ships. Much of this evidence was published, including detailed diagrams showing how slaves were stowed aboard the slave ships. Firsthand evidence about the evils of the slave trade came from Olaudah Equiano, who had been kidnapped in Africa as a child, but had been able to buy his freedom in the Caribbean. He later wrote about his experiences in *The Interesting Life of Olaudah Equiano*.

Kidnapped as a boy in Africa, Olaudah Equiano bought his freedom, became a leading abolitionist, and wrote his autobiography. He insisted on using his African name rather than the slave name, Gustavus Vassa, given to him by his first owner.

William Wilberforce

William Wilberforce was a wealthy man whom John Newton, the former slave trader who became a clergyman, had persuaded to join the Society for the Abolition of the Slave Trade. Wilberforce soon became its leader. In 1788 he wrote:

> *The main object I have in view is the prevention of all further exports of slaves from Africa.*

Supported by evidence gathered by abolitionists that graphically illustrated the suffering of captives on the Middle Passage, Wilberforce worked hard to persuade Parliament to make it illegal to participate in the slave trade. However, slave traders and plantation owners had too many friends and allies among Members of Parliament, and Wilberforce's arguments failed to win the support of a majority of MPs.

As a consequence, the Society and its supporters stepped up their campaign for the abolition of the slave trade, and the abolitionists published even more horrific accounts of what happened on the Middle Passage and on plantations in British colonies. The pottery manufacturer, Josiah Wedgwood, produced china goods decorated with the Society's seal to publicize its campaign and raise funds for the abolitionist movement.

William Wilberforce (1759–1833) was 30 years of age when he began to campaign against the evils of the slave trade. As a Member of Parliament, he was able to put forward his arguments to the British government for the next 18 years.

Slave Revolt in Saint-Domingue

Meanwhile, events in the Caribbean were taking a different turn. In 1789 the French people overthrew their king, and in 1793 executed him. On the Caribbean island of Saint-Domingue, the slaves soon followed the revolutionary example of their French masters and, following a bloody revolt, attempted to abolish plantation slavery. Saint-Domingue's slaves burned down plantations and slaughtered slave owners and their families. A total of 10,000 colonists fled to other colonies in the Caribbean and North America.

Jean-Baptiste Belley

In 1791, when the French National Assembly had decided to extend the Revolution's Declaration of the Rights of Man to include freed slaves and their descendants, but not slaves, French colonists forced the government to back down. Three years later, a former Haitian slave from Saint-Domingue named Jean-Baptiste Belley, who was a deputy to the National Convention in Paris, made an impassioned speech that pledged Haitian loyalty to the cause of Revolution, but asked the Convention to abolish slavery. The Convention decreed that:

all men, without distinction of color, domiciled in the colonies, are French citizens, and enjoy all the rights assured under the Constitution.

Belley demonstrated that African captives and their descendants could produce leaders of quality who could match their European counterparts in terms of eloquence and political skill.

Jean-Baptiste Belley was a former slave from Saint-Domingue who spoke at the National Convention in Paris on behalf of African descendants who lived in France's Caribbean colonies.

A Growing Momentum

The liberation of Saint-Domingue (later Haiti) and the freeing of all its slaves had far-reaching consequences in the Americas and Europe. The slave revolutionaries forced the French revolutionaries to tackle the issues of racial equality and slave emancipation. The revolt removed France as a commercial rival to the British in the Caribbean, and contributed to the British decision to abolish their slave trade with Africa. Moreover, the example of the Haitians encouraged slave rebellions in other colonies. Later, the Haitians would provide assistance to General Simon Bolivar in his struggle against European colonization in South America.

In 1791 a former slave named Francois-Dominique Toussaint Breda led the armed forces of the French colony of Saint-Domingue against British and Spanish invaders. Dropping the name Breda, he called himself "L'Ouverture" (French for "opening"), and in 1801 he declared that the colony was an independent state.

The British Relent

Back in Britain, Wilberforce tried every year for nearly two decades to persuade the British Parliament to abolish the slave trade, but failed. However, in 1807 both Houses of Parliament voted to pass a law abolishing the slave trade between Britain, Africa, and all British colonies. British traders and ships could no longer participate in the transatlantic slave trade. In fact, the Royal Navy would try to prohibit other countries' ships from trading in slaves.

In all, 283 British Members of Parliament voted for the abolition of the slave trade, and only 16 voted against. Despite Wilberforce and his fellow abolitionists having fought against the slave trade for more than 30 years, in the end it was political and economic circumstances that finally persuaded their opponents to accept that abolition was in British interests.

The British naval victory at Trafalgar in 1805 ended the threat from the French and Spanish navies, and the British wanted to take full advantage of their sea power. They could stop and search foreign vessels on the pretext of halting the transatlantic slave trade to deprive the French, Spanish, Portuguese, and Dutch colonies, as well as the American states, of new batches of African captives. In the process, they were able to disrupt enemy trade. This took place at a time when British prosperity no longer relied on slave labor in the colonies since domestic industries had developed rapidly. British plantation owners in the Caribbean also wanted to make life difficult for their rivals by ending the slave trade.

British naval supremacy was confirmed at the Battle of Trafalgar, and paved the way for British efforts to bring the transatlantic slave trade to an end.

British Opposition to Abolition

There were many reasons why it had taken so long to persuade Britain's political leaders to abolish the transatlantic trade in African captives. One reason was that the slave trade had many powerful supporters. Plantation owners based in the Caribbean, the merchants who bought their produce, and the absentee plantation owners living in Britain—some of them Members of Parliament—were well organized and influential. They had enough wealth to bribe other Members of Parliament to support them. They also had the support of King George III until he became too ill to influence government policy. Many influential people were prepared to believe that the abolitionists had exaggerated the number of occasions when slaves had been badly treated. They believed that the enterprise of slave-owning planters had helped make Britain wealthy and prosperous.

Wars Against France

Another factor that delayed the abolition of the slave trade was the French Revolutionary Wars. Britain had joined an alliance of countries that had gone to war against the new republican government of France. This conflict did not end until 1815, when Napoleon was defeated at the Battle of Waterloo. These wars made heavy financial demands on Britain, and most politicians believed that ending the slave trade would be too costly. It was also claimed that the transatlantic trade was an essential training ground for the Royal Navy that defended the British Isles from invasion.

Napoleon (1769–1821), Emperor of France, embarked on a series of wars against other European states. These wars had repercussions for European colonies in the Caribbean, as well as in North and South America.

The Effects of British Abolition in the United States

Agriculture in the American South relied on slave labor. Once the British began to bring the legal trade in African captives to an end, slave trading between states grew in scale and profitability. As plantation farming in the upper South declined in states such as Maryland, Virginia, North Carolina, and South Carolina, demand for slaves grew in states where cotton plantations were making large profits. As the *Charleston Mercury* noted before the Civil War:

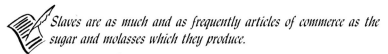 *Slaves are as much and as frequently articles of commerce as the sugar and molasses which they produce.*

Slave traders were everywhere in the South. Some companies had branch offices in towns and cities throughout the slave states. They advertised in newspapers, offering high prices for fit and healthy slaves, and visited farms and plantations to offer owners cash for slaves who would fetch good prices at auction. New Orleans was the largest slave-trading center in the Deep South, handling slaves from the upper South who were sold to the thriving cotton and sugar-growing areas.

The internal slave trade within the United States led to untold suffering within the African-American community. In the decades before the Civil War, as slave traders sought to maintain profit margins, it was common for families to be split up and sold as individuals to the highest bidder. It was not unusual for husbands to be sold separately from their wives, and for parents to be separated from their children. A former slave, Josiah Henson, described how as a young child:

My brothers and sisters were bid off first, one by one, while my mother, paralyzed by grief, held me by the hand.

The inhumanity of slave ownership and the trade in human beings is illustrated by this poster. It lists people for sale, giving their age, physical attributes, and details of any skills or training that will increase their value to a potential purchaser.

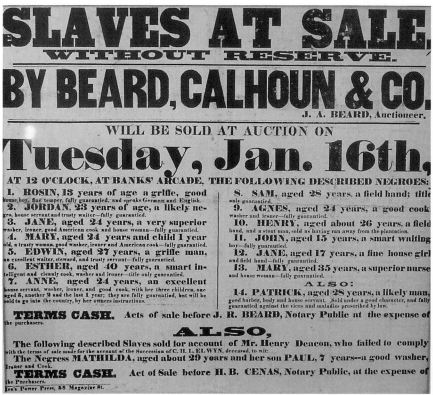

THE ABOLITION OF SLAVERY IN THE U.S.

Revolts and Sabotage

The most common form of resistance to slavery was called "silent sabotage." Many slaves expressed their discontent by vandalizing owners' property and stealing food and other objects from the masters and their families. Whenever possible, gangs of field hands opposed efforts to impose a strict routine on their working day. The result was that most gangs tended to work long hours at a leisurely pace, interrupted by short periods of intense activity, often carried out under the threat of the master's whip. Few field hands were forced to work on Sundays, and some owners felt obliged to pay their slaves to work on the Sabbath at harvest time.

The most extreme form of resistance to the institution of slavery in the South was confrontation. Slaves would offer physical resistance to whites in extreme circumstances, such as when they were provoked by violent or abusive slave owners or overseers, or threatened by the sale of a family member to another estate some distance away. The few major slave revolts that erupted were local affairs, and they were swiftly crushed by the use of armed force. The most bloody slave revolt in American history took place in 1811, when 500 slaves in Louisiana marched on New Orleans, led by a former slave driver named Charles Deslondes. More than 60 slaves were killed in battle or executed in the aftermath of the rebellion. The most famous slave-led insurrection was Nat Turner's revolt in Southampton County, Virginia, in 1831. Turner held out for two months, until he was captured, tried, and executed.

Runaways

Most successful runaways were young adult males from the states of Maryland, Virginia, Kentucky, and Missouri, fortunate in having less distance to travel to reach the free states in the North. Most fugitive slaves hid out close to their owners' plantations. Some eluded capture long enough to join the free African-American

Many people risked their lives and freedom to assist runaway slaves.

The fact that rewards were offered for the return of runaways suggests that people had to be encouraged to capture slaves who were fleeing from their masters.

$00,00 REWARD!

RANAWAY from the subscriber, on the 10th inst., a Negro Man named Jack, about 35 years of age, about 5 feet 5 inches high, weighs 125 or 130 lbs., dark copper color, some teeth out before, has an impediment in his walk as if he were stiff in the hip joint, his clothing consisted of black cloth pantaloons, blue cloth close bodied coat, and black over coat, boots and over shoes--boots have been lately half-soled;--also a black oil cloth satchel. I will give $25 if taken in the county, or $100 if taken out of the county, or $50 if taken out of the State, or lodged in any jail that I may get him, or delivered to me in Haynesville, Clinton County, Missouri.
TAYLOR HULEN.

March 12, 1858.

population in the larger towns, but most runaways were captured. Persistent truants could expect to be brutally beaten or maimed, but even runaways who simply took off to visit friends or relatives, or escape censure for some minor misdemeanor, would be fortunate to receive no more than verbal abuse from their owners.

Some runaways received food and shelter from sympathetic people whom they met on their journey, and others were guided by around 3,000 "conductors" who broke the law to assist runaways on the so-called Underground Railroad. It has been estimated that possibly 75,000 slaves escaped to freedom using this network of routes north from the slave states. The fugitive slave Harriet Tubman is credited with having conducted at least 300 runaways to freedom, including escorting a group of eleven fugitives to freedom in Canada.

Maroon Communities

A small number of escaped slaves formed groups of fugitives known as "maroons," who lived in inaccessible swamps in Florida, remote sea islands in South Carolina, and unsettled areas of Georgia. Sometimes the maroons would attack plantations and take slaves back with them to enlarge their communities.

Early American Abolitionists

In the early years of the American republic, anti-slavery ideals were popular in northern and southern states. Many recognized the conflict between the ideals of the republic's constitution and the harsh realities of slave life. Slavery did not sit well with liberal, humanitarian beliefs, and many Americans had been influenced by the radical social and political ideas that came out of Revolutionary France. Other Americans saw the conflict between slave ownership and Christian beliefs. This period saw a rapid and irreversible decline in the number of slaves in the northern states.

By the early 19th century, the rapid economic development of southern agriculture and the fact that plantation production exploited large numbers of slave laborers appeared to push anti-slavery organizations into the background. A key figure in reviving the abolitionist movement was William Lloyd Garrison, who founded the anti-slavery newspaper *The Liberator* in 1831. In 1833 the American Anti-Slavery Society was founded, demanding immediate emancipation without compensation to slave owners. Within a few years, membership in the Society's 1,500 branches was believed to stand at 250,000 in the northern states.

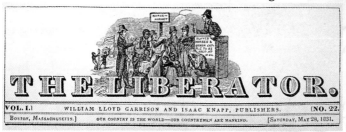

The masthead of William Lloyd Garrison's abolitionist newspaper *The Liberator*, 1831. This newspaper published stories of successful runaways and provided details of slave owners' abuses of their slaves.

Frederick Douglass, a runaway slave who became an agent for the Anti-Slavery Society, traveled widely in the North, lecturing against slavery and campaigning for the rights of free African Americans. He published the first of three autobiographies, *The Narrative of the Life of Frederick Douglass: An American Slave* in 1845. To escape recapture he sailed to Britain, and in 1846 British friends purchased his freedom from Hugh Auld, his former owner.

Many people in the North were abolitionists because they believed that slavery was cruel and inhuman. Some opposed slavery because of the harm that it did to whites in slave-owning areas. They believed that it encouraged cruelty to other humans by brutalizing owners and overseers, while poor whites who did not own land or slaves found it difficult to find work, and became lazy or turned to crime.

Harriet Beecher Stowe's novel appealed to hundreds of thousands of Americans in the free states who sympathized with the plight of the novel's African-American hero.

This illustration, dating from 1852, shows one of the novel's characters, George, handing out certificates of freedom to his slaves. Note how the artist has chosen to portray the slaves' reaction to this news in a most undignified manner.

Uncle Tom's Cabin

In March 1852, Harriet Beecher Stowe published her novel *Uncle Tom's Cabin*. She based this work on stories of runaway slaves, and set out to persuade her readers that the evils of slavery had to be ended immediately. Around 100,000 copies of the book were purchased in its first week of publication, and more than two million copies were bought within two years. Other anti-slavery novels had been published before, including Richard Hildreth's *The Slave, or the Memoirs of Archy Moore* in 1836, but *Uncle Tom's Cabin* tapped into a new mood. Mary Chesnut, the wife of a plantation owner, complained in her diary in 1862:

People (in the North) expect more virtue from a plantation African than they can find in practice among themselves.

Emancipation Plans

Some Northerners feared the results of emancipating slaves, while others opposed granting freed African Americans political equality. Consequently, some Northerners supported the idea of setting up colonies of former slaves in either Central America or West Africa, rather than encouraging former slaves to become citizens of the United States. Most Northerners opposed the spread of slavery into the western territories, and this increased political tensions between free and slave states.

Sectionalism

Southerners feared that the North would try to forbid slavery in the West, and both "sections" became concerned at the possibility of a shift in the balance of power between North and South. The Missouri Compromise of 1820, with the admission of Missouri and Maine, balanced the number of slave-owning and free states, which limited discussion about the spread of slavery into the West for a generation.

The 1850 Compromise was supposed to solve the problem of California entering the Union by allowing it to become a free state, so long as stricter laws were passed to make it easier to return escaped slaves to their owners. The Kansas–Nebraska Act of 1854 tried to allow both states to join the Union, so long as both held a referendum to decide whether either would be a slave-owning or a free state. This attempt to find a compromise led to violence and bloodshed.

Tensions between free and slave states grew, and in 1857 the decision of the Supreme Court in the Dred Scott Case concerning the ownership of a runaway slave appeared to extend the rights of slave owners into the free states. In 1859 the abolitionist John Brown tried to initiate a slave revolt in Virginia, and the whole issue of slavery and states' rights went on to dominate the presidential election the following year.

John Brown's attempt at a slave revolt ended in failure. Here, Union soldiers are bringing Brown's followers out of the engine house at Harpers Ferry.

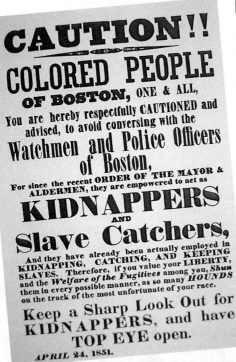

CAUTION!!
COLORED PEOPLE
OF BOSTON, ONE & ALL,
You are hereby respectfully CAUTIONED and advised, to avoid conversing with the
Watchmen and Police Officers of Boston,
For since the recent ORDER OF THE MAYOR & ALDERMEN, they are empowered to act as
KIDNAPPERS
AND
Slave Catchers,
And they have already been actually employed in KIDNAPPING, CATCHING, AND KEEPING SLAVES. Therefore, if you value your LIBERTY, and the Welfare of the Fugitives among you, Shun them in every possible manner, as so many HOUNDS on the track of the most unfortunate of your race.
Keep a Sharp Look Out for KIDNAPPERS, and have TOP EYE open.
APRIL 24, 1851.

This 1851 poster illustrates some of the national tensions. It warns fugitive slaves to stay away from watchmen and police officers in the Boston area who were acting as kidnappers and slave catchers.

National Tensions

By 1860 national politics were sectional, and politicians and parties reflected the widening gap between North and South over the issue of slave-holding in the western territories. Questions about territorial expansion and economic growth, such as the further development of the railroads, were viewed from two different perspectives. Increasingly, many Northerners believed there was a pro-slave conspiracy that influenced the actions of the executive branch and decisions taken by the courts. Many Southerners were convinced that the institution of slavery could be preserved only by secession from the Union.

Abraham Lincoln

When the Republican candidate, Abraham Lincoln, was elected President in 1860, many Southerners were convinced he would try to abolish slavery. Starting with South Carolina, Southern states voted to secede from the Union. In March 1861 the Vice President of the newly-formed Confederacy said:

> our Confederacy is founded upon...the great truth that the black is not equal to the white man. That slavery, subordination to the superior race, is his natural and normal condition.

Lincoln believed that slavery was morally wrong and against the spirit, if not the letter, of the Declaration of Independence and the other ideals of the founding fathers. He opposed the expansion of slavery into the western territories, but he was not an abolitionist at that time. In 1861 he said:

> I have no purpose, directly or indirectly, to interfere with the institution of slavery.

Following his election victory, Lincoln was not convinced that the secessionists in the South would carry out their threat to divide the Union, but he was careful not to say or do anything that would heighten the crisis.

Abraham Lincoln (1809–1865), President, 1860–1865.

The Civil War

Lincoln was not prepared to allow the Southern states to set up a separate Confederacy. The President's primary war aim would be to preserve the Union, not to abolish slavery. As late as August 1862, he wrote:

What I do about slavery, and the colored race, I do because I believe it helps to save the Union....

The war aims of the Confederacy were to preserve slavery, and to fight a defensive war against invasion from the North. As the war progressed, the South hoped to force the North into negotiating a truce that would recognize southern independence. To achieve these aims, the Confederates had to defeat the Union forces in the East, the West, and at sea. The Confederates also hoped to enlist support from the Great Britain and France.

In the east, the fighting centered on northern Virginia, the Shenandoah Valley, Maryland, and Pennsylvania. In the west, the fighting took place in Tennessee, Georgia, and along the Mississippi River. The war at sea focused on Union attempts to blockade Confederate ports and restrict southern trade with other countries, and Confederate attempts to prevent the Union forces from combining their military forces to capture ports and fortresses on important rivers. The first major battle of the war took place at Bull Run near Washington, D.C., in July 1861.

A contemporary illustration of the Battle of Bull Run in July 1861. People in the northern states took great interest in news of the campaigns and battles of the Civil War, which often took place hundreds of miles to the south and west.

War and Freedom

From the beginning of the war, Lincoln's generals had to deal with those slaves freed by advancing Union forces. In 1861 General Benjamin Butler, who commanded a Union army base in Virginia, declared that three fugitive slaves who had escaped from a Confederate labor battalion were enemy property liable to be seized, or "contraband of war." He gave them food, shelter, and work and, within two months, there were about 1,000 contrabands at his base. Later in the same year, General John C. Fremont, who commanded the Union forces in Missouri, issued a proclamation declaring that the slaves of every rebel in the state were free.

Emancipation Proclamation

In September 1861, Lincoln modified Fremont's proclamation so that it freed only those slaves used directly in the Confederate war effort. However, it was not long before Lincoln recognized the strategic value of emancipating all slaves in enemy territory. In 1863 Lincoln's Emancipation Proclamation meant that the abolition of slavery had become one of his government's war aims. As commander-in-chief, the President declared that all slaves in rebel territory were:

thenceforward, and forever free.

The Proclamation did not free any slaves, since slaves living in the four slave states loyal to the Union, and in Confederate territory captured by the Union armies, were not included in the terms of the document. What the Proclamation made clear was that the North was fighting for a Union freed from the moral burden of slavery.

Emancipated slaves traveling north following Lincoln's proclamation in 1863. This fictional scene exaggerates the number of freed men and women who headed north from Confederate territory to the free states.

On The Road to Emancipation

W. T. Sherman (1820–1891), general of the Union army in Georgia and South Carolina, 1864–1865, in heroic pose.

At the end of 1864, General William T. Sherman issued Special Field Order Number 15, granting the Carolina Sea Islands and all of the fertile plantation land 30 miles inland, from Charleston to Jacksonville, to freed slaves. General Rufus Saxton, who commanded the Union occupation forces, settled more than 40,000 freed slaves on this land until Lincoln's successor, President Andrew Johnson, pardoned the rebel landowners and returned their property to them.

Despite the success of the Union campaign after 1863, most slaves were not emancipated until the Confederacy had been defeated. Although more than 500,000 contrabands escaped to freedom behind Union lines, more than three million slaves continued to work on southern farms and plantations throughout the Civil War. The Confederate war department drafted thousands of slaves to work as laborers for the army, and many other slaves accompanied their masters to war as servants. However, many slaves gave food, shelter, and other aid to Union prisoners of war trying to escape from Confederate custody. Besides working as free laborers, contrabands assisted Union troops by supplying them with local intelligence, and the absence of owners and overseers serving in the Confederate armed forces reduced the contribution of slave labor to the southern economy.

In January 1865 the Thirteenth Amendment to the United States Constitution was passed, abolishing slavery in every state of the Union and emancipating nearly four million African Americans. Within four years, the Fourteenth and Fifteenth Amendments and the Civil Rights Act of 1866 confirmed the voting rights and civil rights of the freed slaves.

Reasons for Union Victory

The Union's superior economic resources contributed to the defeat of the Confederacy. Another factor was the collapse of the Confederate forces' supply system, and the subsequent weakening of southern morale in the face of Union advances. This led to a flood of desertions from the southern armies in the later stages of the war. In addition, President Lincoln had a firm grasp of strategy and knew that defeating the Confederate army was more important than occupying the southern territory. To achieve this end, in 1864 he appointed Ulysses S. Grant as General-in-Chief to command his armies. In sharp contrast, Jefferson Davis as Confederate leader failed to convince the southern people that he could lead them to victory.

A Union victory parade held in Washington, D.C., on May 23,1865. The victorious North celebrated the defeat of the Confederacy, rather than the emancipation of the slaves.

The Contribution of African Americans

The contribution of African Americans to the Union war effort had made possible the defeat of the Confederacy. A total of 10,000 African Americans served in the Union navy from the outbreak of the war. At the end of 1862, Lincoln authorized the enlistment of freed slaves into the Union army. More than 190,000 African Americans served in the Union armed forces. They made up nearly 10 percent of enlisted men and received equal pay from 1864 onward. Despite racial prejudice, nearly 100 African Americans were commissioned in the army, and 17 African-American soldiers and 4 sailors received Congressional Medals of Honor. The rebels did not authorize the enlistment of slaves into the Confederate army until March 1865, and they had surrendered before a regiment of slave troops could be organized.

A proud soldier who escaped from slavery to join the Union army. This illustration appeared in *Harper's Weekly* magazine in 1864.

African-American Culture

The ending of the legal slave trade with Africa and the rest of the Americas led to a decline in the influence of African culture on American slaves after 1800. Instead, their shared, common experiences as enslaved rural laborers became important. The movement of slaves within the country, due to the domestic slave trade that developed when the slave trade with Africa ended, also helped to create a common culture among slaves in the South.

Elaborate slave marriage and funeral ceremonies marked key stages in human existence. Slave children grew up listening to similar fables and folk tales told throughout the South. Great respect was accorded to the preachers, folk doctors, midwives, musicians, and storytellers who served the African-American slave community, and who helped to develop a distinct African-American identity before the outbreak of the Civil War.

Measured in thousands rather than millions, some freed slaves marked their emancipation by moving west, where they constructed railroads, worked on cattle ranches, and claimed their own homesteads on the Great Plains. It was not until the 20th century that millions of African Americans abandoned their rural traditions and headed north to live and work in the northern urban centers.

The defeat of the slave states in the Civil War opened the way for the westward expansion of the railroad network. Some African Americans took the opportunity to move west, but the main feature of this development was the destruction of the tribes who lived on the Great Plains.

African-American Abolitionists

In the decades before emancipation, some of the most effective spokespersons for the abolitionists were runaway or former slaves, such as Frederick Douglass, J. W. Loguen, Sojourner Truth, William W. Brown, and Henry H. Garnet. In 1843 Garnet announced to the Convention of Free People of Color, in New York:

Remember that you are four millions! Let your motto be resistance, resistance, RESISTANCE!

African-American abolitionists wanted to shape their own destiny. They had no desire to be the beneficiaries of the paternalism exhibited by their abolitionist allies, such as William Lloyd Garrison and John Brown. Frederick Douglass tried, but failed, to persuade John Brown not to attempt his raid on Harpers Ferry in 1859.

Sojourner Truth (c.1797–1883), a former slave who became a Christian preacher and abolitionist. Like so many African- American abolitionists, her work was overlooked by historians until the second half of the 20th century.

Frederick Douglass (c.1818–1895) became such a famous runaway abolitionist that a song was composed in his honor by Jesse Hutchinson in 1845.

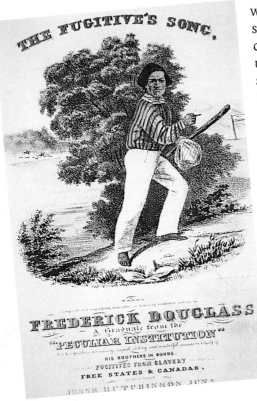

Black Codes

In the American South, the original Black Codes had been introduced as early as 1680 to prevent slave rebellions, but these laws were developed to control every aspect of slave life. Plantation owners, their overseers, their friends and relatives, as well as local townspeople and police, served in patrols set up to enforce the codes in their area. Plantation owners usually paid for the patrols, and failure to serve in one led to a fine. Each patrol was mounted on horseback, armed and accompanied by dogs, and headed by a captain. The patrols could seize and punish any slaves whom they considered to be absent from their plantations without permission, or guilty of breaking the local curfew for African Americans. Slaves who tried to resist the patrol could be shot, and patrols could enter slave cabins to search for weapons, or simply to intimidate the African-American community. After emancipation, it was easy for racists to adopt the patrol model and use it as an effective method of shutting off African Americans from most avenues of freedom and self-expression.

PART III: THE LEGACY

THE EFFECTS OF ABOLITION ON AFRICA

Seeking Alternatives

British sailors chasing a slave trader's dhow, or yacht, near Zanzibar in East Africa. European states tried to bring the African slave trade to an end during the second half of the 19th century.

The long-standing trade in slaves across the Saharan region in Europe and Asia did not increase sufficiently to replace the lucrative export of slaves across the Atlantic. Attempts to preserve the transatlantic slave trade meant dealing with illegal traders who were often unable or unwilling to guarantee steady profits for African merchants. Compared to trading captives, the total value of exports of palm oil, timber, gold, and other products to Europe and the Americas was small. Some West African states developed their own plantation agriculture, using slaves to produce rice, coffee, and cotton. A significant success was the spread of peanut or groundnut cultivation for export, from the Senegal River region to Sierra Leone. Another positive development was the growth of the cocoa industry on the West African Gold Coast in the 1860s.

However, within 40 years, many small trading stations had become huge European colonies that incorporated former independent African states. Sierra Leone and Liberia became colonies for small communities of former slaves. Around 13,000 African Americans had settled in Liberia by 1867. By the end of the 19th century, the British colony of Sierra Leone controlled around 16,500 square miles of territory, and the British colony on the Gold Coast expanded to take control of the Ashanti Confederation and the extensive Northern Territories. Within 40 years, the tiny British colony of Lagos had grown to include most of present-day Nigeria, the second largest state in Africa today. The West African colonies of other European states grew in a similar fashion during this period.

European Paternalism in Africa

The modern map of Africa, with its regular boundaries drawn along lines of latitude and longitude, bears little or no relation to the boundaries of ancient kingdoms and empires. Instead, it is a product of 19th-century European aggression. Many Europeans perceived the failure of so many African economies to find alternatives to the slave trade as a clear sign that Africans were somehow less advanced than themselves. The long and brutal history of African servitude in the Americas had encouraged many Europeans to adopt a paternalistic attitude toward Africa that justified its subjugation and colonization, so long as it was accompanied by the expansion of Christian missionary activities.

A map of Africa pre-1914, showing the imperial acquisitions of European states.

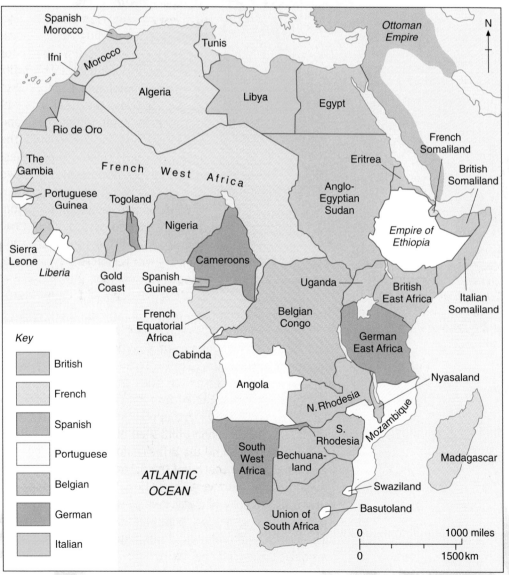

Key
- British
- French
- Spanish
- Portuguese
- Belgian
- German
- Italian

Spanish Morocco
Ifni
Morocco
Tunis
Algeria
Libya
Egypt
Ottoman Empire
N
Rio de Oro
French Somaliland
The Gambia
French West Africa
Eritrea
British Somaliland
Portuguese Guinea
Togoland
Nigeria
Anglo-Egyptian Sudan
Empire of Ethiopia
Sierra Leone
Liberia
Gold Coast
Spanish Guinea
Cameroons
Uganda
British East Africa
Italian Somaliland
French Equatorial Africa
Belgian Congo
Cabinda
German East Africa
Angola
Nyasaland
N. Rhodesia
Mozambique
S. Rhodesia
South West Africa
Bechuana-land
Madagascar
ATLANTIC OCEAN
Swaziland
Basutoland
Union of South Africa

0   1000 miles
0   1500 km

This attack on Dahomey, a coastal region of West Africa, by French troops in 1892, involved the murder of a large number of Africans. Africans were no longer needed as captives, but those who survived these attacks became subjects of European states.

"Scramble for Africa"

The destruction of independent African states in West Africa in the decades following the European withdrawal from the slave trade was repeated in the European conquest of North, South, and East Africa. African resistance provoked brutal reprisals to safeguard European colonists. In the second half of the 19th century, African resistance to European aggression provoked even more European conquest. European states expanded existing colonies, founded new colonies, or established protectorates where the land was not occupied by another European state, but the territory was recognized as being in that state's sphere of influence.

European Rivalry

In Europe, participation in what became known as the "Scramble for Africa" was regarded as a defensive act. European states believed that their African colonies had to be protected from economic competition from the colonies or protectorates of other European states, as well as attacks from local Africans and their rulers. At that time, there were intense political and economic rivalries between European states that made them desperate to acquire new African colonies and extend existing colonies, often simply to prevent territory falling into the hands of rivals. One British politician wrote in 1892:

We are to effect the reconquest of Equatoria and occupy the Albert Lakes and the whole basin of the Upper Nile. Why? For fear of the French, the Germans, the Belgians etc, etc.

Technological developments in 19th-century Europe meant that African armies could do little more than delay the advance of European armies into the interior of the continent. Europeans tried to temper this aggression by claiming that they were striving to wipe out African slavery, and Africa's slave trade with Asia.

European Colonies in Africa

The British, long established in Cape Colony on the southern tip of Africa, extended their colonies in West Africa, seized territory in East Africa, gained control over Egypt—which had been under Ottoman Turkish rule—and dominated Sudan. The French took over most of West and equatorial Africa, as well as Madagascar in East Africa. The Portuguese established their control over Angola and Mozambique, while Spain ruled the northern part of Morocco and the area of Western Sahara. Germany took territory in southwest Africa and East Africa, now known as Namibia and Tanzania, and Italy established colonies in what are now Libya, Eritrea, and Somalia. An African poet in Ghana wrote in 1900:

> *"We've come to trade!!" they said,*
> *"To reform the beliefs of the people,*
> *To halt oppression here below, and theft,*
> *To clean up and overthrow corruption,"*
> *Not all of us grasped their motives,*
> *So now we've become their inferiors.*

Tippu Tib, a powerful African slave trader in the 1880s, grew very wealthy from the sale of captives and ivory to other traders. Tippu Tib's lands were conquered by a Belgian army and made part of the Congo Free State.

Rubber Terror

King Leopold II of Belgium personally controlled the Congo Free State from 1885 to 1908, a vast territory that was bigger than the United Kingdom, France, Germany, Spain, and Italy combined. In this protectorate, all suitable land was divided between concession companies. In rubber-growing areas, forced labor, hostage-taking, brutal beatings, chain gangs, and the destruction of whole villages were employed to subdue and control the African population. These atrocities, committed in the name of the ruler of a small European state, highlight how far the balance of power in Africa had shifted in favor of European colonists.

Similar forced labor systems for extracting rubber were in place in the French territories west and north of the Congo River, in Portuguese-ruled Angola, and in German-controlled Cameroon. African refugees who fled across the Congo River to escape Leopold's ruthless regime often fled back to escape the French brutality in Congo-Brazzaville, and the population loss in this region was nearly 50 percent within 20 years. The "rubber terror" was one of the most barbaric episodes in the European colonization of Africa.

The rule of Leopold II over his personal empire in Africa was one of the most brutal and bloodthirsty episodes in the modern history of Africa.

UP FROM SLAVERY

American Reconstruction

When the American Civil War ended in 1865, around four million American slaves had been emancipated. For the next few years, national politics in the United States were dominated by discussions on the nature and extent of the reconstruction program aimed at the former slave states. This was done without the leadership and guidance of Abraham Lincoln, who had been assassinated at the end of the war.

Legislation passed and ratified by Congress between 1865 and 1870 granted equal civil and political rights to all African Americans. The Civil Rights Act of 1866 defined all persons born in the United States as American citizens with equal rights. The Fourteenth Amendment to the Constitution, ratified in 1868, incorporated the Civil Rights Act's definition of citizenship into the Constitution, and the Fifteenth Amendment, ratified in 1870, declared that:

President Ulysses S. Grant (1822–1885) signed the Fifteenth Amendment to the United States Constitution in March 1870. African Americans soon discovered that laws and constitutional amendments did not guarantee civil rights in a racist community.

the right of citizens of the United States to vote shall not be denied or abridged by the United States or by any State on account of race, color, or previous condition of servitude.

However, in line with the views of most Americans, there would be no major social welfare program to assist freed slaves. As the abolitionist Frederick Douglass said in 1862,

the best way to help them is just to let them help themselves.

Instead, the Freedmen's Bureau was created in May 1865 to distribute food to refugees and the destitute of every race, provide limited health care, establish free labor farming, and assist in the establishment of schools for the children of former slaves. The Bureau's affairs were wound up in 1872.

Sharecropping

Racial prejudices in the South forced the authorities to establish separate facilities for former slaves and their children, often providing inferior services to African Americans. Having freed the slaves without compensating their former owners, the federal government was not willing to go further and confiscate the owners' plantations and redistribute the land to former slaves. However, governments in the South sought to establish a free labor economy, but former slaves celebrated their freedom by refusing to work for overseers or under the gang labor system. As a result, the plantation system of production soon disappeared. Many female former slaves marked their freedom by abandoning fieldwork, and a number of families opted for rental or sharecropping agreements (see below) rather than wage labor. The dream of owning their own land was achieved by some—about 20 percent of African-American families in the former slave states owned their own farms by the end of the 19th century.

The Shore family were African-American homesteaders in Nebraska in 1887. Behind them are the sod houses in which they lived.

This image of an African-American farmstead presents an idealized vision of life in the rural South after the Civil War. In material terms, life did not improve for most freed African Americans for many decades.

Sharecropping became more common in the South in the 1870s. Croppers of any race paid landowners a share of their crop in return for the right to work the land. They used the rest to feed themselves and buy the tools, equipment, seeds, and livestock they needed. In the words of one former slave, sharecropping was more attractive than wage labor since:

I am not working for wages, but am part owner of the crop....

However, for most freed laborers employed in agriculture, whether or not they were sharecroppers, life remained hard.

Buffalo Soldiers

After the Civil War, African-American soldiers who wanted to continue in military service were able to join one of four segregated units in either the Cavalry or Infantry. These units were stationed in the West, where they protected migrants and homesteaders, safeguarded passenger and freight routes, hunted down outlaws, and participated in campaigns against Native Americans, who called them "Buffalo soldiers." During the Spanish-American War, African-American troops served with distinction in Cuba and the Philippines.

Jim Crow

The 50 years before World War I were made more difficult for most African Americans by racist violence and intimidation. The federal government did not act on their behalf when many were prevented from exercising their right to vote. "Jim Crow" segregation laws were introduced to block the path to full citizenship for most African Americans in the South. These laws and rules segregated African Americans from the rest of American society in many states, and denied many their most basic civil rights. Both the National Association for the Advancement of Colored People (NAACP) and the National Urban League (NUL) were founded in this period, to campaign for civil rights and demand that the republic provide:

freedom and justice to all.

Booker T. Washington (1856–1915) was born a slave, but became a teacher and went on to establish his own school, then college, for African Americans at Tuskegee, Alabama.

The Great Migration

By the beginning of the 20th century, the majority of African Americans were literate and many had received degrees from institutions of higher learning. A few, like Booker T. Washington and W. E. B. DuBois, had emerged as national figures in their fight to provide access to education, and full political and civil rights for other African Americans. African-American artistic genius in music, painting, sculpture, literature, and dance was recognized in the United States and Europe. This period also marked the beginning of the Great Migration of African Americans from the rural South to the urban, industrial North in the search of new opportunities.

Marcus Garvey (1887–1940) drives through the streets of Harlem, New York, in a plumed hat and uniform. Garvey was a huge icon for many African Americans.

Marcus Garvey

The Jamaican Marcus Garvey and his Universal Negro Improvement Association (UNIA) represented a crucial phase in the African Americans' struggle for justice and equality. Garvey arrived in the United States at a time of African-American discontent, marked by race riots and racial tension, and he became leader of the largest movement in African-American history. The UNIA incorporated the Black Star shipping line in 1919, to transport passengers between America, the Caribbean, and Africa, and to serve as a symbol of African-American pride and prestige. In 1922 the federal government indicted Garvey on fraud charges. He was imprisoned, and then deported to Jamaica in 1927.

Civil Rights

The stuggle for justice was reignited in the 1950s when Rosa Parks and other African Americans refused to give up their seats on segregated buses in Montgomery, Alabama. They initiated a campaign against the laws that denied African Americans their full civil rights and forced them to use separate but not equal facilities. One of the civil rights campaign's leaders was a preacher named Martin Luther King, Jr., who declared:

Martin Luther King, Jr., (1929–1968), seen here front row, far left, leading a vast crowd at a civil rights rally in 1963.

We have no alternative but to protest.

The African-American boycott of Montgomery's buses led to their desegregation, and this was a significant step toward achieving equality for African Americans in the Deep South. Restaurants and other public places were soon desegregated, and in the 1960s, President John F. Kennedy pushed for African-American students to be taught in desegregated public schools. His successor, President Lyndon B. Johnson, supported new legislation aimed at restoring full equal rights to African Americans, including the right to vote in state and federal elections.

Emancipation and Inequality in the Caribbean

Apart from freedom, emancipation brought few other benefits to freed slaves in most Spanish, Portuguese, French, Danish, and Dutch colonies in South America and the Caribbean. There was no redistribution of land that would have prevented freed slaves, who had little or no education and few transferable skills, from sinking to the lower ranks of society. Economic power rested in the hands of former slave owners. Political power was shared by a small elite that consisted of those who boasted of their European ancestry, and those with a mixed race background that distanced them from the most disadvantaged freed slaves.

Saint-Domingue

The exception was the French colony of Saint-Domingue, where the leaders of a successful slave revolt had declared Saint-Domingue to be an independent republic under its alternative name of Haiti in 1804. When Dessalines, the republic's founder, died two years later, the state was divided between a former soldier named Alexandre Petion, and a former slave who had bought his freedom, Henri Christophe. Between them, these men and their followers created a unique society in the Caribbean. Most slave owners and their families had fled or been killed. The ruling elite consisted of the descendants of liaisons between African slaves and their owners, the extended families of slaves who had been freed before the revolts, and those former slaves who had acted as leaders of the slave revolts between 1791 and 1804 and had been rewarded with positions of power and influence.

A Melting Pot

Following the abolition of slavery, developments in the labor market further complicated the racial composition of former colonies in South America and the Caribbean. Contract or indentured labor immigration led to large Asian populations from India and Indonesia being established in Suriname, Guyana, and Trinidad, and smaller populations being settled in Jamaica and a number of other British Caribbean islands. Large-scale immigration from Spain during the first half of the 20th century further marginalized the African Caribbeans on

These houses in Port of Spain on the Caribbean island of Trinidad remind us that for many of the descendants of the region's slave laborers, poor housing, poverty, crime, and low life expectancy are facts of life.

islands such as Cuba, Puerto Rico, and the Dominican Republic. Post-emancipation society in most former colonies was stratified by race and ethnic background, with former slaves and their descendants, plus the surviving remnants of the region's native peoples, invariably the victims of every form of discrimination and racial prejudice.

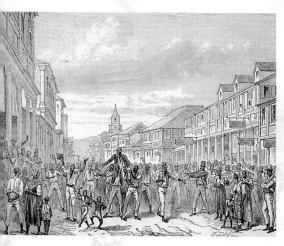

George William Gordon

A demonstration by former slaves in 1865 outside the courthouse in Morant Bay, Jamaica.

In the British colony of Jamaica, George William Gordon, the son of a plantation owner and a slave mother, had urged fellow freed slaves to protest their lack of education and employment opportunities, but in peaceful and nonviolent ways. In 1865 the British put down an uprising of former slaves and their families, and the Governor announced that he held Gordon responsible for the trouble, although he had not taken part in the uprising. Gordon was tried for treason and hanged. It was clear that the world's leading imperial power was not prepared to listen to appeals for racial equality made by some of their Caribbean subjects. Society in British Caribbean colonies was to remain hierarchical and authoritarian for decades, based on ethnic and racial origins inherited from slave times.

Modern Slavery

Angola

Since the abolition of chattel slavery in the Americas, the term *slavery* has been used to refer to a wide variety of human rights violations and slavery-like practices throughout the world. In many places, including Africa, forced labor or debt bondage became a modern form of slavery that continues to blight millions of lives today.

At the beginning of the 20th century, in the huge Portuguese colony of Angola in West Africa, a system of voluntary contracts for paid labor allowed Portuguese traders, known as labor agents, to bargain with local chiefs. In exchange for guns, ammunition, rum, and other goods, the chiefs would ensure that men, women, and children were handed over to plantation owners to be employed as forced labor. Henry W. Nevinson published details of this trade in 1906, and pointed out that for colonists:

the only motive for slavery is money-making, and the only argument in favor of it is that it pays.

In 1961 there was a rebellion against the system of forced labor, followed by a Portuguese campaign of terror that led to the deaths of at least 20,000 Africans. Guerrilla warfare against Portuguese rule lasted for more than 20 years until Portugal granted the colony its independence in 1975. However, various forms of forced labor or bondage exist in Africa and throughout the rest of the world today, despite legal efforts at national and international levels to abolish these practices.

Angolan rebels undergoing attack training for guerrilla warfare in 1961.

Totalitarian States

Over the past 100 years, totalitarian regimes have not hesitated to use slave labor. In the U.S.S.R., Stalin used millions of political prisoners as slave labor on huge

The Nazis forced tens of thousands of their victims to work at forced or slave labor, such as these inmates of Dachau, one of the earliest concentration camps, established in 1933.

construction projects, making the captives a key factor in his economic plans. The use of forced or "corrective" labor declined after the dictator's death, but it continued to exist in various forms until the collapse of the Soviet Union in 1991. During World War II, the Nazi regime forced hundreds of thousands of Soviet prisoners of war, the inmates of labor camps, and conscripted labor from occupied Western Europe to work as slave laborers in factories, mines, and farms. According to the historian Milton Meltzer, by 1944 the Nazis had used more than seven million slaves, who were:

 degraded, beaten, and starved, and often left to die for lack of food, clothing, and shelter.

In China, Mao's "reform through labor" program forced victims of the communist regime into labor reform camps in order to work on major construction projects and produce cheap consumer goods for export.

Modern Slavery

The United Nations defines slavery as the exercise of ownership by one person over another. This can take many forms. Member states of the UN are bound to eradicate chattel slavery, serfdom, debt bondage, the exploitation of children, servile forms of marriage, forced labor, and every form of sexual slavery. African nations whose populations were depleted by the slave trade have considered asking for compensation for centuries of exploitation and forced labor inflicted by European states and their former colonies.

Poverty-stricken children wait for food in a refugee camp. Throughout the world, hundreds of thousands of people have become refugees to escape the horrors of civil war.

Poverty

Evidence from the International Labor Organization, human and civil rights groups, and other investigations confirms that slavery and slavery-like practices can still be found in the world today. A common factor linking most forms of forced labor or servitude is the extreme poverty endured by so many people, whether they are agricultural laborers displaced by debt, war, or climate change, or refugees fleeing political or ethnic conflict or natural disaster. Parents are often involved in slave traffic, abandoning or selling their children to traders. They hope that their sons and daughters will be employed as domestic servants or learn a useful trade, but are aware that they could become young victims of the sex industry.

Child Slavery

Despite laws passed against child slavery in many nations, it has been reported that millions of children are employed as slave or forced labor in factories and workshops in the Indian subcontinent. Children as young as 6 or 7 can be forced to work for 14 hours per day in textile factories. They are frequently beaten, and are too terrified of what might happen to them if they run away from the employer who paid their parents for their bonded labor. In South America, forest clearance and other environmentally destructive enterprises often use debt bondage to obtain labor. Impoverished rural workers are allowed to run up debts to pay for their transportation to the remote forests where they have been promised work. Their wages are held back to pay for debts owed to the company for equipment, accommodation, and food.

Throughout the world, modern lightweight weapons have enabled children to be used in combat as child soldiers. Many children have been used by armed forces as spies, messengers, servants, and prostitutes. Some children have been kidnapped and recruited forcibly into armies and guerrilla groups, but others have been driven into the military by poverty and abuse at the hands of employers and occupying forces. Some governments and armed groups use children because they believe that they are easier to condition, with or without the use of alcohol and drugs, into unthinking obedience. Most child soldiers are between 14 and 18 years of age, but many are recruited from the age of 10 or even younger. Girls and boys are at risk of rape, sexual harassment, and abuse.

Boys training as guerrillas at a secret base in Eritrea represent the modern face of slavery for many children. These boys have had little or no say in their adoption by the soldiers who control their lives, and who could order them to their deaths in battle.

Global Economics

Pressure groups have expressed concern at what they regard as the abuse of power by the world's leading nations, and the growing poverty in many nations, as governments, multinational companies, and world bodies globalize capital and economic development. Campaigners have tried to encourage consumers to boycott goods produced by forced or bonded labor, and turn concern into action against exploitative labor practices and their consequences for the health and welfare of their victims.

Distance and primitive communications allowed 18th-century consumers to ignore the horrors of slavery and the slave trade. Consumers in the 21st century, however, have knowledge about the horrors of modern slavery at their fingertips, due to the revolution in communications technology that has taken place since the 1970s.

David Livingstone (1813–1873) worked as a child in a Scottish textile mill, and went on to become a Christian missionary who campaigned against the horrors of the African slave trade in the second half of the 19th century.

Who Bears the Blame?

In the 19th century, Christian missionaries and explorers, such as David Livingstone, wrote accounts of their expeditions into the African interior and raised public awareness in Europe and North America of the atrocities committed by slave traders. These missionaries, confident of their moral superiority over Africans, worked to abolish slavery and the slave trade, and reshape African society to the European model by supporting the colonization of Africa.

At the beginning of the 21st century, a number of South American, Caribbean, and African states called for the United Nations to declare colonialism and slavery to be crimes against humanity. They also demanded reparations, or compensation, for the long-term effects that slavery and colonialism have had on so many regions. They accused the United States and many European countries of being largely responsible for the poverty and racial tensions that have blighted so many lives.

In response, some former colonial powers claimed that the horrors of slavery and the slave trade were not region-specific. They used as evidence the long-established slave trade between Africa and Asia. States opposed to the demand for reparations suggested that they would be prepared to acknowledge a moral obligation to those countries that suffered from slavery and colonization. Several former colonial powers said that some, but not all, aspects of colonialism had been damaging. This suggests that there are still some changes to be made before paternalistic attitudes toward Africa and South America are done away with in some parts of Europe and North America.

GLOSSARY

abolitionists supporters of various campaigns to end the slave trade or slavery

bills of exchange bills that traders received for slaves, which could be exchanged for cargoes of plantation produce that would fetch high prices in Europe

Black Codes laws originally introduced to prevent slave rebellions, but by the time of American independence had developed to control every aspect of slave life

colony an area of land that another country controls, and often settles in, with or without the full cooperation of the area's original population

Confederacy the Confederate States of America, set up by the states that seceded from the United States in 1861, but defeated in 1865

contrabands slaves living in territory captured by Union forces, or runaway slaves who reached Union forces during the American Civil War; war contraband was any enemy property that was captured by military action

dysentery a disease causing severe diarrhea that often killed African captives on the Middle Passage, due to the effects of dehydration

emancipation the setting free of slaves

Enlightenment 18th-century intellectual movement that believed that rational, critical study and analysis should be applied in all matters

feudal rights a medieval landlord's right to service in the form of work, goods, or other duties

gang system a system of field labor on large plantations in which gangs of slaves perform various tasks according to their age, fitness, and skills

guerrilla irregular, often ill-trained soldiers who use ambush and hit-and-run tactics against better-trained, more powerful opponents

indentured servants servants who signed a contract that bound them to work for a master for a set number of years in return for food and shelter, and possibly training or transportation to a colony

Jim Crow a term to describe the vast number of laws, rules, and regulations that segregated African Americans from other Americans in the years following the American Civil War, up to the 1960s

maroons freed slaves and runaways in remote regions of the Americas who maintained their independence from the slave-owning communities close to where they lived

Middle Passage the journey undertaken by African captives to the Americas by ship

plantation a large area of land on which a single crop, such as sugar, tobacco, or cotton, is grown

Reconstruction the program of aid directed at the defeated Confederacy at the end of the American Civil War, in the hope that the former slave states could be restored quickly to full membership in the Union

republic government without a monarchy, but by an appointed or elected head of state

sectionalism the division of communities or political life along rigid lines based on a single issue that forces groups to ignore what they have in common with each other

serfdom a medieval form of forced labor, where farm laborers and their families worked for a landowner, had few legal rights, and were not allowed to leave their place of work without the permission of the landowner

sharecropping a form of agriculture in which tenant farmers promised a share of their next crop to their landowner in return for credit to purchase seeds, tools, and other resources

slave driver an assistant to a slave owner or overseer, who supervised the work of a slave gang; often, the driver was a trusted slave who received privileges for performing this role

slave overseer an assistant to the slave owner who supervised the work of the slave drivers and the slaves

smallpox an infectious disease that was common in Europe during the 19th century, and caused the deaths of millions throughout the world until it was eradicated in the second half of the 20th century

staple one of the main or usual crops grown in a particular area

trading factories fortified settlements where European merchants traded with local merchants and traders, guarded by European and local troops

transportation a form of punishment by which convicted criminals are used as forced labor in a colony or settlement for a set number of years

Underground Railroad an informal network of more than 3,000 sympathetic people who broke the law by assisting slaves to escape to freedom in the northern states and Canada

TIMELINE OF EVENTS

1492	Christopher Columbus makes landfall in what would become known as the Caribbean or West Indies
1500	Portugal takes possession of Brazil
1655	Jamaican slaves form first large maroon community
1761	Society of Friends bans people engaged in the slave trade from membership
1772	British ruling against forcing a runaway slave to leave Great Britian
1787	Free African Society forms, U.S.; Society for the Abolition of the Slave Trade founded, Great Britain
1791	Extension of French Declaration of the Rights of Man to include freed slaves and their descendants, but not slaves; slave revolt in Saint-Domingue
1794	Slavery abolished in all French colonies
1802	Napoleon I restores slavery in all French colonies
1804	Saint-Domingue declares its independence
1807	British end slave trade in British ships
1815	Most leading European states affirm their opposition to the slave trade
1820	Missouri Compromise
1831	Nat Turner's slave revolt
1833	American Anti-Slavery Society founded
1834	Slavery abolished throughout British Empire

1848	All slaves freed in the French and Danish colonies
1854	Kansas–Nebraska Act
1857	Dred Scott Case
1859	John Brown's attempt at slave revolt in Virginia
1861	American Civil War begins
1863	Emancipation Proclamation
1865	American Civil War ends; Thirteenth Amendment to the U.S. Constitution; British put down a rising of former slaves in Jamaica
1866	Civil Rights Act
1885	King Leopold II of Belgium takes personal control of the Congo Free State; Europe's major powers agree to guidelines for the further colonization of Africa
1886	Slavery in Spain's colonies ends
1888	Slavery abolished in Brazil
1890	17 major powers agree to put an end to African slavery
1944	Seven million Nazi slaves held in concentration camps
1945	United Nations established
1950s	Labor reform camps in China; American civil rights campaigns
1961	Rebellion against forced labor in Angola
1964	Martin Luther King, Jr., awarded Nobel Peace Prize
1975	Angolan independence
1991	U.S.S.R. collapses, ending forced labor in Soviet Union

BOOKS TO READ

Of the thousands of books about the transatlantic slave trade, slavery in the Americas and its abolition, and the aftermath of abolition in the 19th and 20th centuries, the following are among the best starting points:

Drescher, Seymour, and Stanley L. Engerman, eds. *A Historical Guide to World Slavery*. New York: Oxford University Press, 1998.

Eltis, David. *Economic Growth and the Ending of the Transatlantic Slave Trade*. New York: Oxford University Press, 1997.

Haskins, James. *Bound for America: The Forced Migration of Africans to the New World*. New York: Lothrip, Lee, & Shepard Books, 1999.

Jackson, Dave. *Escape From the Slave Traders (Trailblazers Books)*. Minneapolis, MN: Bethany House Publishers, 1992.

Kolchin, Peter. *American Slavery*. New York: Hill and Wang, 1994.

McPherson, James M. *Battle Cry of Freedom: The Civil War Era*. New York: Ballantine Books, 1989.

Meltzer, Milton. *Slavery: A World History*. New York: Da Capo Press, 1993.

Newman, Shirlee P. *The African Slave Trade (Watts Library: History of Slavery)*. Danbury, CT: Franklin Watts Inc., 2000.

Worth, Richard. *Cique of the Amistad and the Slave Trade in World History (In World History)*. Berkeley Heights, NJ: Enslow Publishers Inc., 2001.

INDEX